CONFRONTING INEQUALITY

CONFRONTING INEQUALITY

HOW SOCIETIES CAN CHOOSE INCLUSIVE GROWTH

Jonathan D. Ostry,
Prakash Loungani,
and Andrew Berg

Foreword by Joseph E. Stiglitz

COLUMBIA UNIVERSITY PRESS / NEW YORK

COLUMBIA
UNIVERSITY
PRESS

Columbia University Press gratefully acknowledges the generous contribution
for this book provided by Publisher's Circle member Michael R. Yogg.

The views expressed in this book are those of the authors and do not necessarily
represent the views of the IMF, its Executive Board, or IMF management.

Columbia University Press
Publishers Since 1893
New York Chichester, West Sussex
cup.columbia.edu

Library of Congress Cataloging-in-Publication Data
Names: Ostry, Jonathan David, 1962– author. | Loungani, Prakash, author. |
Berg, Andrew, author.
Title: Confronting inequality : how societies can choose inclusive growth /
Jonathan D. Ostry, Prakash Loungani, and Andrew Berg.
Description: New York : Columbia University Press, [2019] | Includes
bibliographical references and index.
Identifiers: LCCN 2018035788 | ISBN 9780231174688 (hardback) |
ISBN 9780231174695 (pbk.) | ISBN 9780231527613 (e-book)
Subjects: LCSH: Income distribution. | Equality—Economic aspects. |
Economic development.
Classification: LCC HC79.I5 O85 2019 | DDC 339.2—dc23 LC record
available at https://lccn.loc.gov/2018035788

Columbia University Press books are printed on permanent and durable
acid-free paper.
Printed in the United States of America

Cover design: Lisa Hamm

To our wives: Rachel, Gail, and Katie

―⸺∞⸺―

And our children:
Daniel and Joshua, David and Jonathan, and Sarah and Noah,
in the hope that their world will be more inclusive than ours

CONTENTS

FOREWORD

Textbooks in economics often sketch a world in which some people earn more than others because they contribute more to society. In this world, income inequality is thus a just outcome, the result of each getting a reward commensurate to productivity, and redistribution of incomes from the rich to the poor would hurt economic efficiency by taking away incentives for people to work hard. In this fairy-tale world, everyone gets richer over time through increases in productivity.

The reality is otherwise, and in recent years, has been grim. Historically, wages and median incomes have increased in tandem with productivity, but for the past three decades among many rich societies, productivity has increased while median incomes have been stagnant. Labor's share of income has fallen, not just in rich countries, but in many others as well. This suggests that giving capital greater freedom to move within and across countries, while labor remains much less mobile, has led to a weakening of the bargaining power of workers and labor unions. When capital is highly mobile, companies can threaten to move elsewhere if workers don't accept lower wages. If this is so, then wages no longer correspond to workers' marginal contribution to society.

This book shows that, far from being either necessary or good for growth, inequality leads to weaker economic performance. And redistribution of incomes, unless very extreme, does not harm growth. We used to think that there was a trade-off: we could achieve more equality, but only at the expense of overall economic performance. It is now clear that, given the findings of this book and others, greater equality and improved growth go together.

The authors also show that the increase in inequality has been a choice, not an unexpected outcome. The extent of inequality depends very much on the policies governments chose—whether to have unfettered mobility of capital, how much austerity to impose, how much to deregulate markets. These policies may confer growth benefits in some cases but many are shown to have increased inequality over the past three decades.

These conclusions come from careful research conducted by the authors over several years and published in leading academic journals. They represent a welcome commitment at multilateral institutions to evidence-based policy advice. Two decades ago, the IMF was a forceful advocate for allowing free flows of capital across countries. The evidence on the elusive growth benefits of free capital mobility—and on the adverse consequences for both growth and equity when mismanaged opening to capital flows leads to financial crisis—has led to a more nuanced institutional view. And the OECD, which once upon a time advocated a no-holds-barred approach of "Going for Growth" has come around now to thinking that we are all "In It Together: Why Less Inequality Benefits All," the title of its 2015 report.

The policies needed to lower inequality are not difficult to identify. First, we need to keep extreme inequalities of income from emerging in the first place. For this, we need more investment in public goods, particularly health and education, which is a key determinant of workers' income. If governments ensure equal access to health and education, the distribution of incomes will indeed reflect to a much greater extent the distribution of abilities, as the textbooks promise.

Second, we need macroeconomic and structural policies that maintain aggregate demand and deliver full employment. This means monetary and fiscal policies that do not make a fetish of inflation and fiscal targets at the expense of employment and wage growth. It also requires checks on deregulation and capital mobility to tilt the playing field back toward labor. These policies, together with a range of forceful structural policies contributing to the increased bargaining power of workers, improved corporate governance, and taming market power, will go a long way toward redressing the increases in inequality from policy choices over the past three decades. But they may not be enough. So, third, we need to be open to policies to redistribute incomes, as IMF managing director Christine Lagarde noted forcefully at Davos in 2017.

Through these new rules of the road to govern the market economy, it is possible to maintain aggregate demand and thereby alleviate inequality and boost growth. This book's bottom-line message is simple: societies are free to choose policies that will deliver this more inclusive growth.

Joseph E. Stiglitz

PREFACE

I n December 2010, Tunisia erupted in popular protests that brought a swift end to its political regime. This came as a surprise to many, including at the IMF, given the country's sound macroeconomic indicators and the progress it had made in its reform agenda. The events in Tunisia fueled the "Arab Spring," a demand across the region for greater economic equity. In September 2011, the protest against inequality jumped shores with the launch of the Occupy Wall Street movement—their slogan was "We are the 99 percent."

In Washington, in meetings with top staff, the IMF managing director asked in essence: "Why did no one see this coming?" And, more challengingly, management asked how the IMF could be part of the conversation on issues that were rapidly becoming front-page news. The IMF—as an international financial institution with a mandate to promote growth and greater global integration—was not obviously equipped to take on issues such as rising inequality and the demands of the 99 percent.

But our reading of the newspaper headlines reminded us of research we had done on how inequality can be a trigger for derailing a country's growth. Our response to the managing director was to suggest that we draw implications from this research to help IMF country teams better assess a country's growth performance, particularly the sustainability of that performance. Management's encouragement led to the first in the series of papers that underpin the research described in this book. Our finding that inequality leads to fragile growth brought the study of inequality squarely into the domain of the IMF's mandate to promote sustained growth in its member countries.

After that first paper, we branched out on two research fronts. If inequality was detrimental to growth, it was important to figure out both what causes inequality and what could be done to redress it. Surprises awaited us on each front.

On the first question—the causes of inequality—we were expecting that, as conventional wisdom had it, the main underlying causes would be trade and technology. Indeed, these two forces do contribute to inequality. But the research showed that inequality is due as well to the choice of macro-economic policies and structural reforms, on which the IMF itself provides advice to countries. When governments tighten their belts, for instance, through spending cuts or tax increases, inequality goes up. The message is not that such policies should be abandoned, but that countries and the IMF should be aware of these distributional impacts and design their policies to lower such impacts.

On the second question—what to do about inequality—conventional wisdom again led us to expect that steps to redress inequality would end up hurting growth. But we found that redistribution, unless extreme, does not hurt growth. It is good to try to address some of the root causes of excessive inequality, for instance through more equal access to health care and quality education. But these policies cannot work overnight and, even in the longer run, may still not reduce inequality as much as countries may desire. Hence governments should be more open to the use of redistribution as a cure for excessive inequality.

We are gratified that our research findings have made a difference in how the IMF views inequality and in how many people outside the IMF now view the institution. Far from thinking of inequality as removed from the IMF's concerns, our colleagues are now being encouraged to mainstream it in their work—and there is much greater emphasis today in the day-to-day work of the IMF on confronting excessive inequality and protecting vulnerable groups. And many outside the IMF are starting to see what was previously concealed—the human face of the institution. As Christine Lagarde recently remarked: "Reducing high inequality is not just morally and politically correct, it is good economics."

We are grateful to many who have helped us in undertaking the research that underlies the book: our coauthors—Laurence Ball, Edward F. Buffie, Davide Furceri, Siddharth Kothari, Daniel Leigh, Charalambos Tsangarides,

Yorbol Yakhshilikov, Luis-Felipe Zanna, and Aleksandra Zdzienicka; our research assistants—Hites Ahir, Zidong An, Jun Ge, and Suhaib Kebhaj; and colleagues at many institutions who commented on drafts on the key papers—Kaushik Basu, Olivier Blanchard, Sam Bazzi, François Bourguignon, Jamie Galbraith, Doug Gollin, Stephen Jenkins, Aart Kraay, Paul Krugman, Andy Levin, Branko Milanovic, Martin Ravallion, Dani Rodrik, Mark Shaffer, Frederick Solt, Joe Stiglitz, and Larry Summers. While the research was carried out as part of our day jobs, the task of putting together the book took up evenings and weekends: we conclude by thanking our families for putting up with the loss of time together.

CHAPTER 1

INTRODUCTION

I n 2014, Oxfam made headlines with a striking statistic: eighty-five of the world's richest people had more of the world's wealth than the poorest half of humankind—some 3.5 billion people. Former U.S. President Barack Obama called addressing such disparities "the defining challenge of our time." In one of his speeches, Obama noted that "research has shown that countries with less inequality tend to have stronger and steadier economic growth over the long run" (2011).

The research that Obama cited came from the authors of this book and thus from an unlikely source, the International Monetary Fund (IMF). Traditionally, mainstream economists—including those at the IMF—have worried far more about whether average incomes are growing and much less about how that growth is distributed among people. In the jargon of the profession, economists have been more concerned with efficiency—making sure the size of the pie keeps getting larger—than with equity, the size of the slice that goes to each person.

In fact, economists generally frown on too much redistribution—that is, on transferring too much of the pie from the rich to the poor, say by taxing the rich at a much higher rate than the poor or by giving the poor excessive cash transfers and other social benefits (e.g., food stamps and welfare payments). The market, it is felt, gives people their just rewards, and tinkering with these outcomes too much is both unfair and costly over the longer term because it takes away people's incentives to work hard. In other words, economists have argued that too much of a concern with equity would end up hurting efficiency. The IMF's advice to countries on economic policies has generally adhered to this consensus, placing the institution at odds with organizations such as Oxfam that have long called for greater attention to inequality and its consequences.

Over the past decade, however, the research staff of the IMF has done—even in the eyes of its critics such as Oxfam—fundamental work on the costs and causes of inequality and on what can be done to cure excessive inequality. This book draws on this academic research, explaining it in such a way that the key findings can be understood by a broader audience.

There are three important results from our work. The first, the one cited by Obama, is that inequality in incomes is harmful for sustained economic growth. There has been much anguish expressed over inequality in recent years: some find extreme inequality morally repugnant, others worry about the social costs or about political capture by elites—that is, attempts to use their wealth to change rules and regulations in their favor. We do not deny the importance of these reasons to worry about inequality. Our finding of a direct *economic* cost provides an additional powerful reason to be concerned about inequality.

Second, virtually every policy touted by mainstream economists to raise average incomes also has an impact on inequality: it generates winners and losers within countries. Hence, economic policies pose what economists refer to in their jargon as a trade-off between efficiency and equity. Governments have to balance the efficiency gains of making the average person better off with the equity costs of increasing income gaps between the rich and the poor. Our first finding adds a double whammy: the increase in inequality from economic policies can itself detract from durable growth, the very thing that economic policies are trying to foster in the first place. The overall message is not that pro-growth policies should not be pursued, but rather that governments should take steps to redress the policies' impact on the distribution of income. One way is to design economic policies so that the distributional impacts are tempered in the first place. Another remedy is redistribution: using taxes and transfers to redistribute income from the rich to the poor.

Our third finding is that the economic costs of redressing excessive inequality through such redistribution are not necessarily high. There is often a fear that using redistribution to redress inequality may itself cause substantial harm to economic growth—"the cure may be worse than the disease"—because it lowers incentives to work hard. This fear turns out to be misplaced. This book will present evidence showing that redistribution, unless extreme, does not hurt economic growth. It can thus be a win-win policy in many cases: it helps equity without much (or any) adverse impact on efficiency.

Overall, we see these three findings of our book as making a strong evidence-based case for taking inequality seriously and more actively embracing redistribution as a cure. First, inequality causes economic harm by lowering growth and making it less durable. Second, the benefits of most economic policies are not equally shared—and many in society actually lose out due to policies that may be good on average. Third, lowering inequality through redistribution is typically not bad for growth.

ILLUSTRATING EFFICIENCY AND EQUITY

Nobel laureate Robert Lucas of the University of Chicago expresses well why mainstream economists elevate concerns about efficiency over equity. On the importance of growth in incomes, Lucas says:

> Is there some action a government of India could take that would lead the Indian economy to grow . . .? If so, what exactly? The consequences for human welfare involved in questions like these are simply staggering: once one starts to think about them, it is hard to think about anything else. (1988)

But on distribution—and redistribution—Lucas says:

> Of the tendencies that are harmful to sound economics, the most seductive, and in my opinion the most poisonous, is to focus on questions of distribution . . . [Of] the vast increase in the well-being of hundreds of millions of people that has occurred, virtually none of it can be attributed to the direct redistribution of resources from rich to poor. The potential for improving the lives of poor people by finding different ways of distributing current production is nothing compared to the apparently limitless potential of increasing production. (2003)

To illustrate this view, figure 1.1 shows the annual income of the average person in the United States and Brazil from 1950 to 2014. Both panels of the

FIGURE 1.1:   **Average Incomes in the United States and Brazil, 1950–2014**

Average incomes in Brazil are lower than those in the United States and have grown more slowly over the past three decades.

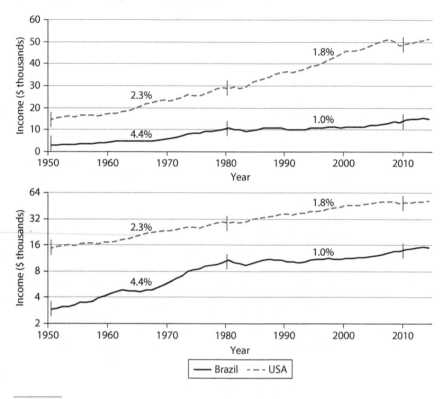

Notes: Both panels of the chart show the same set of data, but the bottom panel uses a log scale, which economists prefer when the data cover a wide range of values. Incomes are adjusted for the effects of inflation; that is, the data shown are for "real" incomes. The percentages 2.3% and 1.8% are the average rate at which U.S. real incomes grew over 1950 to 1980 and 1980 to 2010, respectively; the percentages 4.4% and 1.0% are the corresponding values for Brazil.

Source: Based on data from Penn World Table 9.0.

figure show the same set of data, but the bottom panel is on a logarithmic scale, which is often used when the data cover a large range of values. Two things stand out from the figure. First, the average Brazilian is clearly much poorer: in 2010, for instance, the average income was about $10,000 compared with around $50,000 in the United States. Second, U.S. average incomes have grown at a more steady pace than Brazil's. U.S. incomes grew at 2.3 percent a year between 1950 and 1980 and moderated a bit to 1.8 percent a year between 1980 and 2010. Brazil's growth has been more erratic, with rapid growth of 4.4 percent a year in the earlier period but only 1 percent a year in the later one.

Of course, there are also huge gaps in incomes within the United States and within Brazil. For the United States, the top panel of figure 1.2 shows

FIGURE 1.2: Average U.S. Incomes for the Richest 1 Percent and the Other 99 Percent

In the United States, incomes grew much more rapidly for the top 1 percent than for the bottom 99 percent over 1980 to 2010, in contrast to the pattern over 1950 to 1980.

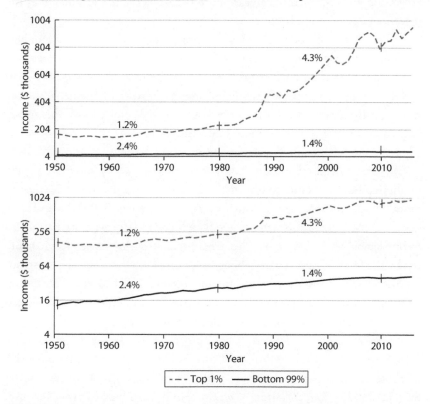

Note: Both panels of the chart show the same set of data, but the bottom panel uses a log scale, which economists prefer when the data cover a wide range of values. Incomes are adjusted for the effects of infla-tion; that is, the data shown are for "real" incomes. The percentages 1.2% and 4.3% are the average rate at which real incomes grew for the top 1 percent over 1950 to 1980 and 1980 to 2010, respectively; the per-centages 2.4% and 1.4% are the corresponding values for the bottom 99 percent.

Source: Based on data from the U.S. Bureau of Economic Analysis.

annual incomes of the richest 1 percent of people and the other 99 percent of the population. In 2010, for instance, the average income among the richest 1 percent was over $800,000 whereas the average income among the rest was $40,000. The virtue of the log scale becomes clearer when we are considering such vast disparities in income. The bottom panel more clearly shows the reversal in income growth rates between the two groups. Between 1950 and 1980, incomes of the bottom 99 percent grew at 2.4 percent a year, twice the rate of income growth of the top 1 percent, perhaps misleading many U.S. economists into thinking that worries about inequality were a thing of the past (Berg and Ostry 2012). In contrast, between 1980 and 2010, incomes at the top grew 4.3 percent a year, more than three times as quickly as the incomes of those at the bottom.

In Lucas's view of the world, these are not particularly disturbing numbers or trends. The gap between rich and poor in the United States is a sideshow compared to the importance of bridging the gap between the average Brazilian and the average U.S. citizen. Yes, U.S. incomes have grown phenomenally at the top, but they have grown for the others as well. Why not cherish this steady improvement in incomes for most U.S. citizens rather than worry about the gap between the bottom 99 percent and the top 1 percent?

There are several reasons offered by those who do worry about inequality. Egalitarian and religious strains of thought simply find extreme inequality morally objectionable. In a famous speech, Pope Francis (2014), for instance, asked for a sharing of the material goods "which God's providence has placed in our hands" and advocated a "legitimate redistribution of economic benefits by the State." Others worry about inequality because of its adverse socioeconomic impacts. Many of these are documented in Richard G. Wilkinson and Kate Pickett (2011). They find that inequality can erode trust in society, increase anxiety and illness, and impede social mobility.

Another reason for concern, noted most powerfully by Nobel laureate Joseph Stiglitz, is that of political capture by elites. "The income and wealth of those at the top comes at least partly at the expense of others," writes Stiglitz (2012). Concentration of wealth can in turn lead to other ills. U.S. Supreme Court Justice Louis Brandeis once observed, "We may have democracy, or we may have wealth concentrated in the hands of a few, but we can't have both." Stiglitz (2015) worries that, in the United States, concentration of income is leading to the formation of oligarchies more interested in preserving their own wealth and power than in fostering societies with equal opportunities for all.

We think these are all important reasons for being concerned about inequality. They are not, however, the focus of this book and hence are not discussed here, except in passing. Our interest is squarely on the economic harm done by inequality by lowering growth and making it less durable. Some years ago, we set out to understand what sustains long periods of healthy growth, which we call in this book *growth spells*. Other economists, notably Lant Pritchett at Harvard University, documented that countries rarely enjoy a steady economic climb (Pritchett 2000). Periods of growth are often punctuated by collapses and stagnation, as we saw in the case of Brazil between 1980 and 2010. Moreover, spurring growth is often not the hard part; even in the poorest regions and in poorly managed economies, growth takeoffs are relatively common. The hard part is sustaining growth spells.

What stood out most from our analysis was that growth spells were much more likely to end in countries with higher inequality. To be sure, many other factors influence the duration of growth spells, but inequality belongs in this pantheon and its effect is large. If Latin America, for example, could bridge half of its inequality gap with East Asia, its growth spells would last twice as long as they do now. To us, this provides a powerful additional reason why inequality has to be taken seriously, even by those—such as Lucas—whose primary concern is about the growth in incomes of the average person. Inequality and fragile growth may be two sides of the same coin.

BALANCING EQUITY AND EFFICIENCY

Economists recommend many policies to countries to help them boost average incomes. These policies are generally grouped under two headings: structural and macroeconomic. The first is a broad group, which includes being open to international trade and flows of foreign capital, avoiding excessive regulation of product and labor markets, and adopting policies to deregulate the financial sector. The second group includes policies by the finance (or treasury) ministries to keep the government's budget deficits—the gap between how much the government spends and how much it collects in taxes—from getting too large and by central banks to keep inflation in check.

There is evidence that many structural policies do contribute to efficiency, that is, they boost average incomes. What we document in this book, however, is that many of these same policies also raise inequality, hence setting up a trade-off between equity and efficiency. Governments have to decide whether the boost in average incomes justifies increasing the disparity in incomes among individuals within the country. Our first result leads to an additional concern: the increased inequality resulting from economic policies can itself undercut the durability of growth, eroding some of the efficiency gains.

The government's decisions are particularly difficult in cases where the efficiency gains are elusive but the equity costs are palpable. We focus on two such policies. First, over the past few decades, countries have increasingly opened up to foreign capital. In theory, such financial openness—or capital account liberalization—allows countries access to a deeper pool of capital and allows the owners of capital to search among a wider set of investment projects. The better matching of capital with investment projects should be good for growth in all countries. An oil exploration company based in an advanced economy, for instance, could help fund projects in a low-income economy where oil had been discovered.

In practice, the benefits of increasing openness to foreign capital have proved elusive, particularly in countries where financial development is low and access to finance is not widespread among the population. In fact, the evidence has been that foreign capital flows have often contributed to rising financial volatility and crises. While the efficiency gains are difficult to establish, the equity costs are not: we document that episodes of significant opening up of the capital account—in Bolivia, Egypt, Nepal, and Uganda, among many other countries—have been followed by increased inequality. Some of this increase in inequality occurs because those who are already well-off are better able to take advantage of the access to foreign capital. Another reason is that the crises that occur in the aftermath of many episodes of capital account liberalization exert a higher toll on the poor.

The second policy we discuss at length is that of governments to lower their budget deficits. Economists refer to such actions as fiscal consolidation; critics refer to these actions as austerity policies. The past few decades have been associated with frequent fiscal consolidations—combinations of spending cuts and tax hikes to reduce the budget deficit. The U.S. Omnibus Budget Reconciliation Act of 1993 is an example of such a policy action. Other examples include the actions by many European countries, such as Austria in 1996, as they sought to meet the budget deficit criteria laid down in the Maastricht Treaty for joining the European Monetary Union.

The evidence shows that these episodes are followed by a decline in average incomes and a rise in unemployment in the short- and medium-run, that is, in the three to five years after an episode of consolidation. There is also an increase in inequality in the aftermath of austerity. This is because cuts in social benefits and public sector wages, often associated with consolidation, disproportion-ately affect lower-income groups. Fiscal consolidations also raise long-term unemployment, and long spells of unemployment are likely to be associated with significant earnings losses.

Of course, fiscal consolidation may confer long-term benefits by keeping the government's books in order: we do not deny this and discuss the pros and cons of paying off government debt when it becomes very high. Our message is that austerity should not be undertaken in the hope of short- and medium-run efficiency gains and that the equity costs should be borne in mind.

REDRESSING INEQUALITY

Some inequality of incomes is integral to a market economy. Without the ability to retain a large part of the fruits of their labor, peoples' incentives to work hard erode over time, as the example of the former Soviet Union poignantly shows. Poorly designed efforts to reduce inequality could also end up lowering incentives to work and invest, and thereby undermine growth, hurting even the poor.

It would thus be a mistake to conclude that policies should always be geared to reducing inequality at the expense of other economic and social goals. The evidence in this book on the costs of inequality shows, however, that ignoring inequality would also be a mistake. Concretely, what could governments do to redress extreme inequality? The first set of steps goes by the label of *predistribution policies.* These are steps that are taken in the hope that extreme inequalities of income do not manifest themselves in the first place. Providing more equal access to education and health care generates equality of opportunity—that is, it raises the odds that the poor and their children end with high incomes despite the disadvantages of their initial starting points in life. What governments choose to do with tax revenues is crucial in this regard: using them to improve access to education and health would be a good predistribution policy.

In addition, policies can be designed with sensitivity to distributional outcomes. In the case of austerity policies, for instance, protecting benefits for the poor from cuts can help counter some of their impact on inequality. In the case of financial openness, governments could choose to sequence policies such that domestic financial development and access to finance (especially by the poor) are improved before opening up to foreign flows of capital—this raises the odds of a favorable impact on both growth and equity, because financial flows are more likely to be intermediated efficiently and because credit is more likely to actually reach all segments of society (genuine financial inclusion).

Despite these attempts, inequality may still end up higher than governments and citizens prefer. Redistribution through taxes and transfers offers a cure after the fact. However, support for redistribution has been held back by the fear that it is bad for growth. The evidence in this book shows that redistribution, unless it is extreme, does not have adverse impacts on growth. Hence, it should remain on the policy menu as one of the cures for excessive inequality.

A ROADMAP TO THE BOOK

Chapter 2 provides an introduction to the measurement and drivers of inequality. We then turn to the costs of inequality, discussing at length our research on the adverse impact of inequality on the durability of growth (chapter 3). The four chapters that follow document the impact of economic policies on growth and inequality, namely structural policies (chapter 4), financial openness (chapter 5), austerity policies (chapter 6), and interest rate policies (chapter 7). The impact of technology, specifically the spread of robots, on inequality is discussed in chapter 8. The book concludes with a discussion of the cures for excessive inequality, particularly the effects of redistribution (chapter 9) and the implications of our research for governments and the international institutions that advise them (chapter 10).

This book is written with the aim of explaining our research to a broad audience; hence technical discussions are kept to a minimum in the main text. But academic economists (and professionals in related fields such as political science) will also find the book of value. In addition to providing a one-stop shop for our research, the book contains a technical appendix at the end with the details needed to understand fully our results.

CHAPTER 2

INEQUALITY: MEASURES AND DRIVERS

Much of the discussion in this book is about the inequality of incomes within countries. Other authors, notably Milanovic (2005), have studied global inequality, that is, the difference between the incomes of the rich and the poor without regard to nationality; this measure of inequality has declined over time, in large part due to rising incomes in populous countries such as China and India. Yet, as Milanovic notes, inequality appears to be on the rise within many countries around the world.

How should we measure the gap between the rich and the poor within countries? This chapter begins by describing the three measures that we use. The first is the Gini coefficient, which is the most widely used—but not the most easily understood—measure of inequality. The second is the share of income accruing to the richest segments of the population, for example the top 1, 5, or 10 percent of the population. The third is the share of income going to labor: the share made up by wages and salaries as opposed to other forms of income such as profits. The chapter concludes with a primer on the drivers of inequality.

Before we get to inequality, however, we have to understand the distinction between market income and net (or disposable) income, which plays an important role in this book. Most societies levy taxes on income and also provide some assistance to people in the form of transfers. Net income is market income adjusted for those taxes and transfers; that is, we subtract from market income the taxes paid on that income and add in the transfers received.

FIGURE 2.1: **Average Market and Net Incomes in the United States and France**

Net incomes are derived from market incomes by subtracting taxes paid to the government and adding in transfers received from the government. The average person pays more in taxes than he or she receives in transfers. (Figures are in 2011 U.S. dollars.)

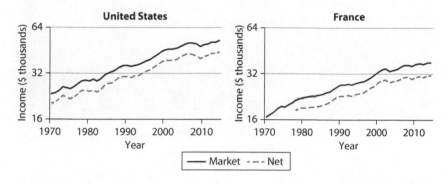

Source: Based on OECD data.

To illustrate the distinction, figure 2.1 shows annual market and net incomes for the average person in the United States and France from 1970 to 2014. For both countries, net incomes are below market incomes. This means that the average person pays more in taxes than he or she receives in transfers. People much poorer than the average are likely to be receiving more in transfers than they pay in taxes; hence, their net incomes would be higher than market incomes, and the opposite would be true for people much richer than the average.

THE GINI COEFFICIENT

Now let's move to comparing inequality in incomes in the two countries. Figure 2.2 shows how market and net incomes in the two countries are distributed across deciles, from the poorest tenth of the population (decile 1) to the richest (decile 10). The height of each bar shows the percent share of income going to that decile. If market incomes were equal across the population, each of the bars shown in the top panel would be of the same height

FIGURE 2.2: Market and Net Incomes by Decile in the United States and France

Less of U.S. income goes to the poorer deciles than in France.

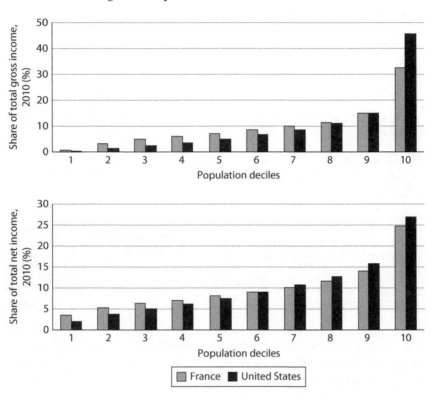

Note: The bars paired are ordered from the poorest 10 percent of the population to the richest 10 percent.

Source: Based on data from World Income Inequality Database 3.4.

and at 10 percent (and indeed the concept of a decile would be redundant). Even if market incomes were not equal, societies could choose, through taxes and transfers, to make net incomes equal, so that the net income bars in the bottom panel would be of the same height at 10 percent.

Of course, in both the United States and France, market incomes are far from equal across the population and so are net incomes, despite redistribution from rich to poor. For example, the share of market income going to the richest decile is about 35 percent in France and about 45 percent in the United States. Redistribution does lower these shares considerably: in both countries, the share of net income going to the richest decile falls to below 30 percent, but it is still well above the 10 percent share of a perfectly equal society.

Is market income inequality lower in France than in the United States? And how does redistribution affect the relative inequality in the two countries? The data in figure 2.2 can inform our answers to these two questions but cannot resolve them fully. Take the question about market inequality: It's true that the share of incomes going to the very poor deciles is higher in France than in the United States, but even the middle-income deciles in France have a higher share than their U.S. counterparts. So, while the gap between the very poor and the very rich seems smaller in France, the gap between upper-middle incomes and the very poor could well be larger.

The second question is also difficult to answer purely from a visual inspection of the data. Redistribution does lower the share of incomes going to the very top, as we already noticed, but it moves it to both the very poor and the middle class, again making the impact on inequality uncertain.

If we were only interested in, say, the gap between the poorest and the richest deciles, we could make statements about the relative inequality in the two countries. But in general, we would like to be able to compare overall inequality in the two countries, not just at particular deciles. Here's where the Gini coefficient comes to the rescue. Technically, the Gini measures the average difference in income between any two randomly chosen people in the population. It thus provides a summary measure of inequality within a country. The index is scaled so that it varies from 0 to 100: 0 means that everyone in society receives the same income and 100 means that one person gets all the income.

Figure 2.3 explains the concept of the Gini coefficient, continuing with the example of France and the United States and using net incomes. The vertical axis cumulates the share of income going to each decile. If income within a country was completely equally distributed, the points would all lie along the 45-degree line and the Gini coefficient would be 0. Now consider what France's data look like compared to the line of complete equality. The poorest 10 percent of the population account for about 4 percent of the income. The next decile gets 5 percent of the income, bringing the cumulative total to 9 percent as shown. We proceed in this manner, adding deciles and showing

FIGURE 2.3: **Gini Index of Net Income in the United States and France in 2010**

The Gini measure provides a summary statistic of the extent of income inequality in a country.

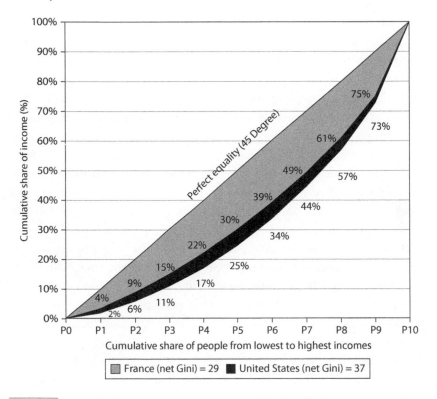

Note: The numbers shown are the cumulative percent shares of net income received by people up to that decile. For instance, "30" and "25" at P5 indicate that the poorer half of the population receives 30 percent of the income in France and 25 percent of the income in the United States.

Source: Based on data from World Income Inequality Database 3.4.

the cumulative totals at each step. The figure also shows similar numbers for the United States.

It is now evident that no matter which decile we consider, the cumulative share of income going to individuals with incomes up to that decile is higher in France than in the United States: there is indeed less inequality, overall, in France than in the United States. The mathematical formula used to compute the

FIGURE 2.4: **Gini of Market and Net Incomes in the United States and France**

Inequality of market incomes is similar in the United States and France. Inequality of net incomes in the United States is much higher than in France and it has also increased over time.

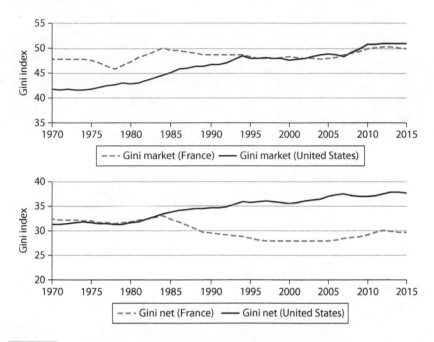

Source: Based on data from the Standardized World Income Inequality Database 6.1.

Gini summarizes this difference between the income distributions of the two countries by giving France a lower coefficient (29) than the United States (37).

Armed with this knowledge about the Gini coefficient, let's return to the discussion of U.S. versus French market and net incomes and see how inequality has evolved over time in the two countries. Figure 2.4 shows the Gini index, computed using both market and net incomes. The top panel gives the striking result that the inequality of market incomes has been quite similar in the United States and France since 1995. What is different in the two countries is the inequality in net incomes, which since 1985 has been much lower in France.

FIGURE 2.5: **Redistributing Income**

Most countries have much lower net inequality than market inequality due to redistribution.

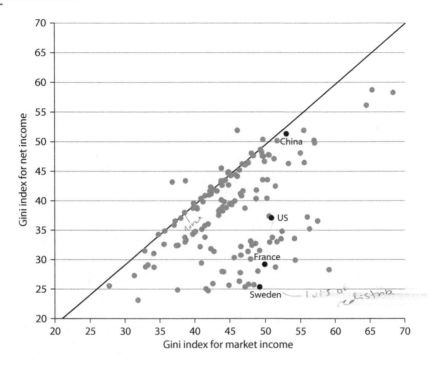

Note: Countries close to the 45-degree line redistribute little; those farther away redistribute more.

Source: Based on data from the Standardized World Income Inequality Database 6.1.

We can compute market and net Ginis for a large group of countries across the world. The results for 2018 are shown in figure 2.5. This figure shows market inequality on the horizontal axis and net inequality on the vertical axis. Each point represents a particular country. A country on the 45-degree line would have identical market and net inequality, implying that no redistribution was being carried out. A country far below this line would have much lower net than market inequality, meaning that a lot of redistribution was taking place.

Almost all countries lie below the line, implying some degree of redistribution. Some, such as China, do little of it; others, such as Sweden, do a lot.

And on average, the distance from the line grows with the amount of market inequality, showing that countries with more unequal market incomes tend to redistribute more. We can verify from the figure that the market income Ginis for the United States and France are virtually the same, whereas the U.S. net income Gini is much higher than that of France.

Table 2.1 shows the countries with the highest and lowest Gini coefficients in 2010 for market and net incomes. It also shows the countries with the largest increases and decreases in inequality between 1990 and 2010.

TOP INCOME AND LABOR INCOME SHARES

Most inequality data, such as those on Ginis that we have been studying, come originally from surveys that typically ask households about income from various sources, taxes, and consumption. Surveys, which are expensive and complex, generally are undertaken only every few years at best. And there is no guarantee that the surveys are representative. The very rich may be less likely to participate or reluctant to reveal the true extent of their incomes in a survey (Ostry and Berg 2014).

Because of these limitations of surveys, economists began looking to tax records as a source of income distribution data (Atkinson, Piketty, and Saez 2011). These data are available for all taxpayers, so the rich are better represented and it is possible to look at small segments, such as the top 0.1 percent. Moreover, the data tend to be available annually and often as far back as the early twentieth century.

But there are also important disadvantages to using tax data. First, the many poor and even middle-class people who do not pay income taxes are excluded. Second, there is generally little information on actual taxes paid and transfers received that allow the calculation of net income. Third, data are available only for advanced economies and a handful of emerging markets. And fourth, tax-based data have their own measurement problems related to misreporting and the use of tax-avoidance strategies, many of which are perhaps particularly available to the richest.

Still, the share of income going to the very top provides a useful complement to the Gini measures. Figure 2.6 shows the share of income going to the richest 1 percent of households in the United States and France. In the 1970s,

TABLE 2.1: Inequality of Market (Gross) Income and Net Income (Income After Taxes and Transfers)

[handwritten annotations: "lots of ineq. bu gov't." | "low ineq. in free mkt" | "little redist" | "lott of redis'"]

High Market Gini (2010)		Low Market Gini (2010)		High Net Gini (2010)		Low Net Gini (2010)	
Country	*Gini*	*Country*	*Gini*	*Country*	*Gini*	*Country*	*Gini*
South Africa	68	Iceland	39	South Africa	59	Czech Republic	26
Zambia	60	New Zealand	39	Zimbabwe	52	Netherlands	26
Zimbabwe	60	Kazakhstan	38	China	51	Ukraine	26
Latvia	57	Tanzania	38	Honduras	51	Belarus	25
Ireland	56	Mali	37	Zambia	51	Belgium	25
Lithuania	56	Fiji	36	Rwanda	50	Denmark	25
Rwanda	56	Ukraine	35	Guatemala	49	Iceland	25
Brazil	54	Taiwan	33	Chile	48	Slovenia	25
Honduras	54	Belarus	32	Colombia	48	Sweden	25
United Kingdom	54	Korea, Rep. of	32	India	48	Norway	24

Largest Increase in Market Gini (1990–2010)		Largest Decrease in Market Gini (1990–2010)		Largest Increase in Net Gini (1990–2010)		Largest Decrease in Net Gini (1990–2010)	
Country	*Change*	*Country*	*Change*	*Country*	*Change*	*Country*	*Change*
Latvia	+33	Sierra Leone	−28	Georgia	+19	Sierra Leone	−24
Lithuania	+31	Malawi	−17	Rwanda	+19	Malawi	−15
Georgia	+22	Senegal	−9	China	+16	Iran	−7
Rwanda	+21	Iran	−8	Latvia	+14	Senegal	−7
Cyprus	+20	Fiji	−6	Lithuania	+14	Brazil	−6
Macedonia	+20	Tanzania	−6	Macedonia	+14	Fiji	−6
Russia	+19	Turkey	−6	Armenia	+12	Tanzania	−6
Estonia	+18	Egypt	−5	Bulgaria	+12	Egypt	−5
Bulgaria	+17	Mali	−5	Cyprus	+12	Mali	−5
China	+16	Peru	−5	Slovakia	+12	Turkey	−5

Source: Based on data from the Standardized World Income Inequality Database 6.1.

FIGURE 2.6: Top 1 Percent Income Shares in the United States and France

The share of income going to the richest 1 percent has risen sharply in the United States but has remained fairly stable in France.

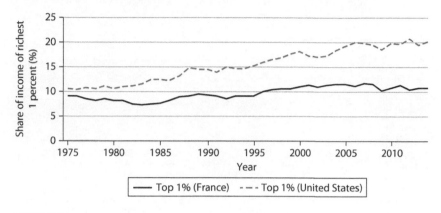

Source: Based on data from the World Wealth & Income Database.

the share was about 10 percent in both countries. Since then, however, the share has increased in the United States so that the richest 1 percent has about 20 percent of total income; in France the share has remained stable.

Another way of looking at the distribution of income is to compute the share that goes to labor compared to capital. As *Washington Post* columnist Robert Samuelson notes, calculating "labor's share is straightforward. It covers workers' wages, salaries and fringe benefits. Capital is more complicated. It includes corporate profits, the income of small businesses and professional partnerships, rents from real estate and net interest on bank deposits, bonds and loans" (Samuelson 2013). Over the past few decades, labor's share of income—the part that is relatively easy to compute—has fallen in many countries. "The shift to capital is worldwide," Samuelson (2013) observes, due to forces such as "globalization, new technologies, and weaker unions. All tend to beat down wages through intensified competition, the substitution of machines for people and the loss of bargaining power."

Figure 2.7 shows labor shares for the United States and France. The U.S. labor income share is much lower today than it was in 1970, about 60 percent compared to 66 percent. France too has seen its labor share decline, though much of it happened during the 1980s.

FIGURE 2.7:   **Labor Share of Income in the United States and France**

The labor share of income has decreased sharply in the United States since 2000 but has remained fairly stable in France.

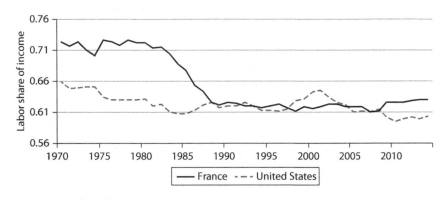

Source: Based on data from the Penn World Table 9.0.

DRIVERS OF INEQUALITY

We conclude this chapter with an exploration into the drivers of inequality. We have carried out a comprehensive investigation of what drives inequality—as measured by the Gini coefficient—using data for ninety countries from 1970 to 2015.

Nobel laureate Simon Kuznets conjectured that inequality would initially increase as a country goes from being poor to middle-income—as it first opens up to the forces of competition—but then decline past a certain threshold level of income (Kuznets 1955). This "Kuznets curve" does indeed explain some of the evolution of inequality across countries and over time. But we find that it also leaves a lot of inequality unexplained. As emphasized by Milanovic (2016), a multitude of other factors account for changes in inequality. In our investigation, we group these into four categories.

Structural factors: As we discussed in chapter 1, inequality of incomes could be due to inequality of opportunity, but the latter is difficult to measure directly. The mortality rate provides a proxy; for instance, higher mortality rates could be an indication of lack of access to health care. Hence, we include the mortality rate as a control for such difficult-to-measure factors that influence inequality of opportunity. The share of industry in gross domestic product (GDP) is used as an indicator for the structural transformation of the economy. Inequality tends to be very high in countries still dominated by agriculture and declines as resources move out of that sector into industry and services.

Global trends: Trends are measured by technology and by openness to trade, both of which have tended to raise inequality in recent decades. Technological change has conferred an advantage on those adept at working with computers and information technology. Global supply chains have moved low-skill tasks out of advanced economies. Thus the demand for highly skilled workers in advanced economies has increased, raising their incomes relative to those less skilled. And often, the people who benefit from these developments in the developing economies tend to be the higher-skilled people in those economies.

Economic policies: We include here (1) the degree of financial openness—the extent to which countries are open to foreign flows of capital, (2) domestic financial reforms, and (3) the size of government—share of government spending in GDP. As noted earlier, we expect that opening up to foreign capital flows raises inequality because the poor do not gain access to foreign capital and lose out disproportionately if opening up is followed by a crisis. Some of the same reasons, for instance lack of access to financial services, could also lead to higher inequality in the aftermath of domestic financial deregulation. Based on our findings on the link between fiscal consolidation and inequality, we expect that shrinking the size of government will raise inequality.

Other factors: Crises are often mentioned as leading to inequality by having a greater impact on the poor than the rich—hence an indicator of currency crises is included. The last variable is a proxy for dictatorial governments (whether the head of government is a military officer), which tend to raise inequality by allowing greater expropriation of wealth by elites.

Each bar in figure 2.8 shows the impact on the Gini from an increase in each of these drivers; in each case the increase considered is an increase in the value of the indicator from the fiftieth percentile to the seventy-fifth percentile of its distribution. The first thing to note is that each set of factors plays a role in

FIGURE 2.8: The Effect on Inequality from a Fiftieth to Seventy-Fifth Percentile Change

Inequality is not driven solely by global trends or structural factors. Economic policies within the control of governments also play an important role.

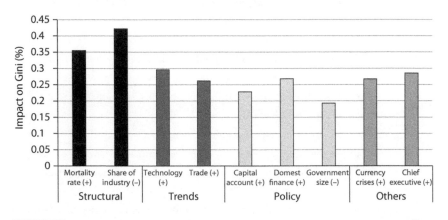

Source: Furceri, Loungani, and Ostry (2018).

contributing to inequality. For example, a country that is more open to trade has a higher Gini coefficient, as does a country that is more open to modern technology. The impact of each of the other factors conforms to our expectations, as discussed above.

For the purposes of this book, the key finding is that inequality is not driven solely by global trends or deeper structural factors: economic policies within the control of governments also play an important role. The three indicators of economic policies we have included, and which will be the subject of chapters that follow, all contribute significantly to raising inequality even after accounting for the influence of several other factors.

It is worth noting that policies toward trade liberalization are also to some extent within the control of governments, though small countries may have little choice but to integrate with others. The impact of currency crises is also to a large extent dependent on policy choices. In short, the extent of inequality that we have attributed to economic policies may be an underestimate.

CHAPTER 3

INEQUALITY AND SUSTAINED GROWTH

There is a long history of academic work on whether inequality affects growth. Boushey and Price (2014) provide an accessible survey of the literature in which they conclude that, while theory points to "numerous possible mechanisms" with "conflicting outcomes," the evidence is now clear: "As new data become available and better data analysis methods are applied . . . studies that look at the longer-term effects find that inequality adversely affects growth."

Previous studies, however, have neglected a key feature of the growth process, which is particularly important in developing countries: its lack of persistence. Average incomes do not typically grow steadily for decades. Rather, periods of rapid growth are punctuated by collapses and sometimes stagnation—the hills, valleys, and plateaus of growth. Relating inequality to medium-run average growth may thus miss the point. The more relevant issue for many countries is whether inequality is related to these sharp growth breaks.

Figure 3.1 shows that the evolution of average incomes in advanced countries, such as the United States and the United Kingdom, is consistent with the common perception that development is similar to climbing a hill: more-or-less steady increases in income, with small bumps along the way. If this were the universal pattern, the most interesting question would be how to explain why some countries grow faster than others over long periods. But the figure also shows that in emerging markets and developing countries—such as Brazil, Cameroon, Chile, and Jordan—there is a variety

FIGURE 3.1: Growth Patterns in Advanced and Developing Countries

The common perception of development as a steady process holds true in some advanced economies (as depicted for the United Kingdom and the United States), but developing countries experience a bumpier process.

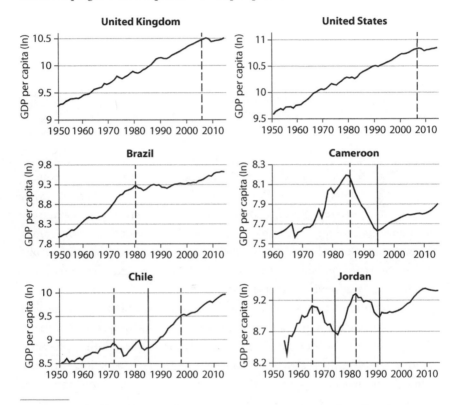

Note: Vertical dashed lines represent statistically significant growth downbreaks; solid lines represent upbreaks. Real GDP per capita is measured on a logarithmic scale, so a straight line implies a constant growth rate.

Source: Berg and Ostry (2017).

of experiences. Looking at such pictures, Pritchett (2000) and other authors have been struck that an understanding of growth must involve explaining why some countries are able to keep growing for long periods of time, whereas others see growth downbreaks after just a few years, followed by stagnation or decay.

The question of how to sustain growth is particularly interesting for two reasons. First, igniting growth has proven much less challenging than sustaining growth (Hausmann, Pritchett, and Rodrik 2005). That is, even the poorest of countries or countries with poor economic institutions have managed to get growth going for several years from time to time. Where growth laggards differ from their more successful peers is in their inability to sustain growth for long periods of time. Second, since the 2000s, a large number of countries have experienced sustained growth. This is particularly the case in sub-Saharan Africa, where many countries had a takeoff in the mid-1990s. Is this growth likely to persist, and how can it be kept going?

MEASURING SUSTAINED GROWTH

We focus therefore on the duration of "growth spells"—starting when growth takes off (the "upbreak") and ending when growth slacks (the "downbreak"). We then try to explain how this duration depends on various policies and country characteristics, including inequality. Because the goal is to examine trends, not temporary events such as recoveries from recessions or booms, we look only at growth spells that have lasted at least eight years.

As we started to pull together the data, it became evident that both upbreaks and downbreaks were indeed quite common. As figure 3.2 shows, upbreaks tend to be fairly spread out across regions and have occurred in every decade. A key message from the data is thus that the initiation of growth is not the hard part of trying to achieve a long-run rise in per capita incomes. Rather, the real problem is the inability to sustain growth over long periods. For example, almost all growth spells in advanced countries and in emerging Asia last at least 10 years or more, but only about two-thirds of Latin American and African spells do (figure 3.1).

Another salient feature of the data is the rate of growth when the country is in a spell versus the aftermath of a spell. As table 3.1 shows, all regions' spells involve fairly fast growth, with those in Africa actually the most rapid. In contrast, there are big differences across country groupings following the end of spells. African spells have tended to end in deep collapses, whereas soft landings have tended to follow the end of growth spells in advanced countries and Asia.

FIGURE 3.2: Growth Breaks by Region and Decade

Upbreaks and downbreaks are quite common and tend to be fairly evenly spread out across regions.

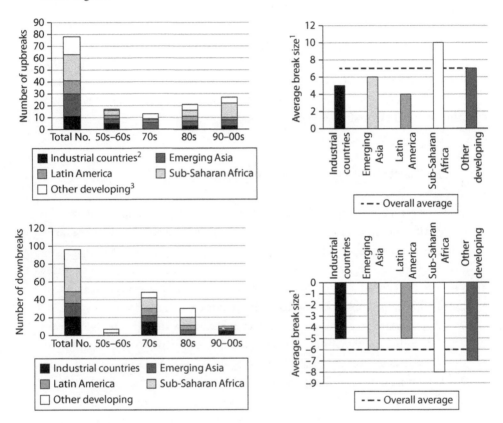

1/ Percentage point change in real per capita GDP growth before and after the break.

2/ Includes Japan, Korea, Singapore, Hong Kong SAR, and Taiwan Province of China.

3/ Middle East, North Africa, Cyprus, Turkey, and Caribbean countries.

Note: A growth break is a statistically significant change in the per capita real GDP growth rate that persists for at least eight years.

Source: Based on Berg and Ostry (2017).

TABLE 3.1: Characteristics of Growth Spells

Region	Frequency and Duration					Average Growth Before, During, and After [1]				
	No. of Countries	No. of Spells	Mean Duration (Years)	% Spells Lasting at Least		Average Growth			3 Years	
				10 Years	16 Years	Before	During	After	Before	After
Complete Spells										
Industrial countries 2/	37	2	13	100	0	3	6	1	2.6	3.4
Emerging Asia	22	3	18	33	33	-0.7	9	1	1	2
Latin America	18	5	14	60	40	1	5	0.2	1	-1
Sub-Saharan Africa	43	3	8	0	0	-3	10	-4	-11	-7
Other developing 3/	20	7	11	43	14	-2	5	-1	-1	-2
Total (including incomplete spells)										
Industrial countries 2/	37	11	24	100	64	0.7	6	N/A	-0.1	N/A
Emerging Asia	22	16	24	88	56	-0.3	6	N/A	0.4	N/A
Latin America	18	7	16	71	43	0.4	4	N/A	0.1	N/A
Sub-Saharan Africa	43	18	14	67	22	-4	6	N/A	-8	N/A
Other developing 3/	20	12	14	67	33	-2	5	N/A	-3	N/A

1/ Real per capita GDP growth, in percentage points.

2/ Includes Japan, Korea, Singapore, Hong Kong SAR, and Taiwan Province of China.

3/ Middle East, North Africa, Cyprus, Turkey, and Caribbean countries.

Note: A growth spell is a period between a growth upbreak and a growth downbreak, as long as per capita real growth is above 2 percent during the spell and falls to below 2 percent after the downbreak. Breaks are at least eight years apart.

Source: Berg, Ostry, and Zettelmeyer (2012).

INEQUALITY AND SUSTAINED GROWTH: THE EVIDENCE

Having identified the growth spells over the last half century, we then turned to the question of how the duration of these spells relates to differences in inequality. Figure 3.3 illustrates the relationship between the duration of growth spells and the Gini measure of income inequality for a sample of countries. There is clearly a promising pattern here: more inequality seems associated with less sustained growth.

This figure is only the starting point of our analysis, however. Many other factors could determine the duration of a country's growth spells: the quality of its economic and political institutions, openness to trade, macroeconomic stability, and the skills of its labor force (human capital accumulation, in the jargon). Our next step therefore is to consider how some of these other factors

FIGURE 3.3: Duration of Growth Spells and Inequality

More inequality is associated with less sustained growth.

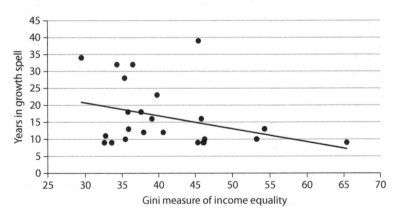

Note: This figure includes spells that end in-sample (completed spells) only, because the length of incomplete spells is unknown. For this figure, minimum spell length is eight years. Countries include Belgium, Chile, Denmark, Dominican Republic, Ecuador, Egypt, France, Greece, Guatemala, Indonesia, Ireland, Jamaica, Japan, Jordan, Malawi, Nigeria, Pakistan, Philippines, Portugal, Republic of Korea, Senegal, Syrian Arab Republic, Taiwan PoC, Thailand, and Tunisia.

Source: Berg and Ostry (2017); updated.

affected the duration of growth spells, and to explore whether inequality still played a role once the impact of these other factors was accounted for.

Our approach borrows from the medical literature that aims to gauge, for example, how long someone might be expected to live conditional on certain factors (whether they smoke, their weight, their gender, their age, etc.). In our context, the probability that a growth spell will end depends on its current length and various "hazards" to growth. The analysis distinguishes between initial conditions at the onset of the spell and changes during a growth spell.

Unfortunately, there are not enough data to test at once all the theories about what could affect growth spells. There are simply too few spells and too many candidate explanations to disentangle everything. Moreover, many of the candidate determinants of spell duration could themselves be correlated with one another. Hence, we did some preliminary analysis to find a set of candidates that appeared to show promise, ones that ended up as important in most samples and specifications. On this basis, we ended up with six factors that played a significant role in explaining the duration of growth spells: (1) political institutions, (2) openness to trade, (3) exchange rate competitiveness, (4) foreign direct investment (FDI), (5) reliance on external debt, and (6) inequality.

The first five of these factors are not much of a surprise given what is already known about the determinants of growth. Each of these factors has been mentioned as being potentially important in that vast literature. Many have argued that political institutions that constrain the executive and secure accountability help growth (Sokoloff and Engerman 2000). There is also evidence that trade liberalization helps growth by increasing market size, promoting competition, and making it easier to transmit know-how (Alesina, Spolaore, and Wacziarg 2005). An overvalued exchange rate can undermine growth by making the manufacturing sector less competitive (Rodrik 2008). And while the growth benefits of foreign capital flows are difficult to establish, as we discuss in later chapters, some flows such as FDI do seem to help growth, as does lower reliance on external debt (Dell'Ariccia et al. 2008).

We find these factors to be also important for the duration of growth spells. The duration is higher in countries that have better political institutions, are more open to trade, maintain a competitive exchange rate, attract more foreign direct investment, and have lower external debt.

Our results show that inequality belongs as a sixth factor in this pantheon of determinants of the duration of growth spells: Countries with a more equal income distribution have longer spells. Inequality retains its statistical and economic significance despite the inclusion of the other factors discussed above. This suggests that inequality matters in and of itself and is not just picking up the effects of other factors. Inequality also preserves its significance more systematically across different samples and definitions of growth spells than the other factors. It is thus a more robust predictor of growth duration than many variables widely understood to be central to growth.

Overall, the results of the analysis support some interpretations of why East Asian economies grew rapidly between 1965 and 1990—a development that has come to be called "the East Asian Miracle" (World Bank 1993). Growth is most enduring in countries that are open to trade, attract foreign direct investment, maintain low external debt, and have relatively equal income distribution. Given this, it is worth noting that our overall results hold up even when Asia is excluded from the sample.

Figure 3.4 provides a view of the importance of each variable. It reports the increase in expected spell duration for a given increase in the variable in question, keeping other factors constant. There is a large and significant association between income inequality and growth duration. A 10-percentage-point decrease in inequality—the sort of improvement that a number of countries have observed during their spells—increases the expected length of a growth spell by 50 percent.

The channels through which income inequality affects the duration of growth can be both economic and political. One economic channel—which economists put under the category of credit market imperfections—is that poor people do not have the means to finance a good education or afford quality health care. Hence, they are unable to build up their human capital and this makes it difficult to sustain the economy's growth. This echoes the arguments in Wilkinson and Pickett (2011) that more unequal countries suffer from relatively poor social and health indicators, such as increased illness and anxiety.

Income inequality may also increase the risk of political instability. In unequal societies, there may be greater tussles between the rich elites and the rest for political power, and the resulting uncertainty could reduce incentives to invest and hence impair growth (Alesina and Rodrik 1994). Beyond this, the ability of unequal societies to respond effectively to adversity may be lower because it may be more difficult to rally everyone to a common cause

FIGURE 3.4: The Effect of Increase of Different Factors on Growth Spell Duration

Many factors increase the duration of growth spells but a more equal income distribution is one of the more important factors.

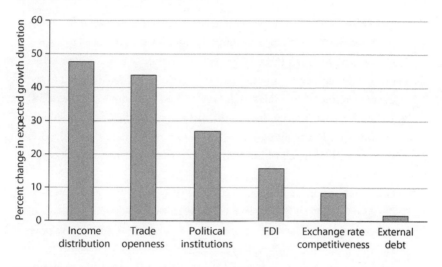

Note: For each variable, the height of the figure shows the percentage increase in spell duration resulting from an increase in that variable from the fiftieth to the sixtieth percentile, with other variables at the fiftieth percentile. For trade, the figure shows the benefits of having an open instead of a closed regime, using the Wacziarg and Welch (2008) dichotomous variable. For political institutions, the figure shows the effects of a move from a rating of 1 (autocracy) to 0.

Source: Berg and Ostry (2017).

(Rodrik 1999, b). This greater difficulty reflects the fact that, in good times, the "have-nots" were left behind; thus, they see little point in supporting the pain of societal adjustment in tough times when the prospects of future gains for them are slim.

THE ENDS OF SPELLS: SOME COUNTRY CASES

Our statistical results on inequality and the duration of growth, and our conjectures about the channels through which these results come about, are reflected in the political and economic narratives of many countries. Table 3.2 lists the six cases where our statistical analysis indicated the risk of the spell ending was the highest among all the countries in our sample. In the economic histories of these cases, we often found mention of the role of income distribution in bringing the spells to an end.

➤ **Colombia** experienced a spell end in 1978. Our statistical model predicts that Colombia's growth spell was indeed fragile—with a risk of ending sixty-six times higher than the average over all the spells in our sample. This higher risk can be decomposed into the six determinants included in the duration results: Colombia's high Gini (53 vs. the sample average of 38) accounts for most of the higher risk. While the spark was a crackdown on drug cartels, beginning a long civil conflict, Cardenas (2007) notes the role of "high levels of inequality and poverty and the weak presence of the state."

➤ **Guatemala** was in a state of civil war from 1960 until 1996. In the words of Thorp et al. (2006): "By the late 1970s, Guatemala had entered a stage of polarization and radicalization of social organizations (trade unions, peasant organizations)." Carbonnier (2002) further notes that "attempts to cut subsidies and raise transportation prices repeatedly spurred violent clashes in the streets of Guatemala City." The prediction of the model is that the risk of Guatemala's spell ending was indeed about fifty-five times higher than the average country during 1974–1979, with higher-than-average income inequality being one of the main factors driving the result.

➤ The ends of spells in **Cameroon, Nigeria**, and **Ecuador** demonstrate how income distribution can interact with adverse external developments. Lewis (2007) notes for Nigeria that highly volatile politics, lack of social cohesion, and external shocks drove bursts of economic volatility: "In Nigeria, ethnic and regional competition has hampered the formation of a stable growth coalition between the state and private producers. Political elites have turned instead to populist strategies and diffuse rent distribution among a fragmented and polarized business class. The populist option proved short-lived when oil revenues dwindled, while the residual rentier alliances were unstable, resulting in economic stagnation and disarray." In Cameroon and Ecuador, oil wealth in the 1970s initially financed large increases in the public sector, particularly in the wage bill, which proved very difficult to cut when oil prices fell. "Although these measures were

TABLE 3.2: The Ends of Six Growth Spells

Country	Spell Dates	Growth in Real Per Capita GDP		Hazard Ratio	Main Contributing Factors (Share of Total Hazard)					
		During Spell	Next Decade		Inequality	Low FDI Inflow	Increased External Debt	More Autocracy	Over-valuation	Trade Liberalization
Cameroon	1978–1985	6.6	−5.6	109	0.49	0.33	−0.05	0.33	0.09	0.11
Colombia	1967–1978	3.4	1.2	66	0.73	0.46	−0.06	−0.23	−0.03	0.12
Guatemala	1958–1979	2.4	−1.3	56	0.39	0.38	−0.07	0.13	−0.02	0.13
Ecuador	1971–1978	7.2	−1.0	47	1.05	0.34	−0.05	0.17	−0.13	−0.07
Panama	1959–1980	4.7	0.0	42	0.44	−0.61	0.62	0.28	0.06	0.14
Nigeria	1968–1976	5.9	−4.0	29	0.27	0.41	−0.08	0.39	0.47	0.15

Note: The hazard ratio is the predicted probability that the spell would end during the five years prior to its actual end, as a ratio to the predicted probability of a spell ending for the average observation in the entire sample. Thus, a hazard ratio of 1 implies no unusual risk that the spell will end. See Berg, Ostry, and Zettelmeyer (2012) and the technical appendix to this book for details.

Source: Berg and Ostry (2017).

necessary to rescue [Cameroon] from further economic crisis, they were very unpopular because they least affected the political elite and those in the upper echelon of government, whose privileges remained intact" (Mbaku and Takougang 2003; see also Jácome et al. 1998 and Aerts et al. 2000). In all three countries, the model's hazard ratio was very high (ranging from more than one hundred times higher than normal for Cameroon to twenty-nine times higher for Nigeria) and high inequality and autocracy levels as well as low levels of FDI, played important roles in bringing the growth spell to an end according to our statistical results.

➤ The model attributes the (high) risk of **Panama**'s spell ending mainly to rising external debt, along with inequality. Indeed, Panama's military dictatorship preserved power through the 1970s increasingly by borrowing externally to support transfers to government workers (Ropp 1992). The global crisis of the early 1980s thus hit Panama hard. This pattern is consistent with the argument in Berg and Sachs (1988) that countries that suffered most from the debt crisis of the 1980s may have been those that used (unsustainable) foreign borrowing to bridge societal conflict.

The variety and complexity of the channels are evident in these examples. The timing of crises seems to reflect an interaction of underlying vulnerabilities, including income distribution. Clearly, ethnic fractionalization plays a role in some cases too. The statistical evidence shows that inequality is an underlying feature that makes it more likely that a number of these factors come together to bring a growth spell to an end.

CHAPTER 4

STRUCTURAL POLICIES
AND INEQUALITY

In January 1982, in his *Newsweek* column, Milton Friedman hailed Chile as an "economic miracle." A decade earlier, Chile had turned to policies—the pursuit of free ("liberalized") markets, a smaller role for the state, and globalization—that have since been widely emulated across the globe.

Figure 4.1 illustrates the global pivot to these policies in the 1980s. There is a strong upward trend in the extent to which countries introduced competition in various spheres of economic activity. Along with the shift to free markets, the size of the state—measured by government spending as a share of GDP—shrank. This smaller role for the state has been achieved through privatization and limits on the ability of governments to run fiscal deficits and accumulate debt. There has also been a steady move toward globalization, most notably in increased freedom for capital to move across national borders. Chile was ahead of the median country in all respects except in capital mobility: it maintained tighter restrictions than others through the 1990s but liberalized more actively later.

With this chapter, we begin our analysis of the impacts of these policies on average incomes and on income inequality. We first study the impacts of various structural policies (or "reforms" as proponents of these policies tend to call them). While the reform index shown in the upper left panel of figure 4.1 is a composite of various policies, in this chapter we will look at the impact of each of the underlying policies separately. We then devote chapter 5 to a further and more detailed analysis of one of these policies—financial openness or capital

Globally there was a strong upward trend beginning in the early 1980s toward adopting policies of deregulation, limiting the role of the state, and financial and trade openness.

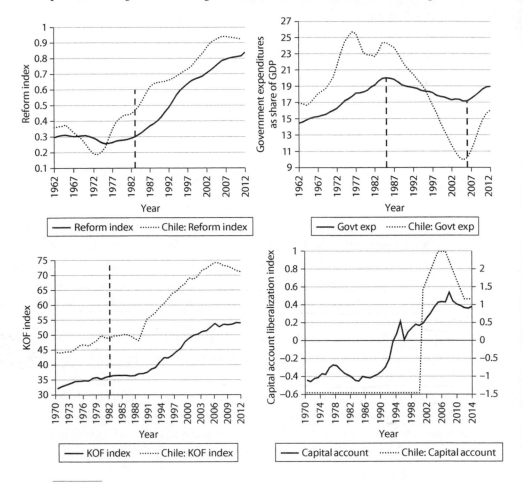

Note: Composite index of policies to increase competition and to deregulate. Index takes values between 0 and 1. The median value across countries is shown. The index is smoothed using a five-year moving average.

Source: Ostry, Loungani, and Furceri (2018).

Note: Government expenditures as a share of GDP (including health and education). The median value across countries is shown. Data are smoothed using a five-year moving average.

Source: Ostry, Loungani, and Furceri (2018).

Note: The Konjunkturforschungsstelle (KOF) globalization index measures the extent that a country is globalized in three dimensions: economic, social, and political. The index ranges from 0 to 100; larger values indicate more globalization.

Source: Gygli, Haelg, and Sturm (2018) and Dreher (2006).

Note: Chinn-Ito index for period 1970–2014. The index takes values between −1.89 (most restrictive) and 2.39 (most open). The mean value across countries is shown. Chile right scale, data on Chile prior to 2001 are an average of the period 1970–2000.

Source: Chinn and Ito (2006).

account liberalization, illustrated in the bottom panels of figure 4.1. Chapter 6 looks at the impact of austerity—the shrinking of the size of the state, shown in the top right panel of Figure 4.1.

MEASURING STRUCTURAL REFORMS

We assemble a comprehensive dataset of seven reform indices, covering both the financial and nonfinancial sectors of the economy (economists tend to refer to the nonfinancial sector as the "real" sector of the economy): domestic finance, tariffs, current account (or trade), capital (or financial) account, network industries, collective bargaining, and law and order.

Each of these indices attempts to measure the extent to which the sectors were deregulated, competition was strengthened, and institutions were improved. To take an example, the index for financial sector reforms—the first item in the list above—is based on the extent of interest rates and credit controls in place (the more controls in place, the more regulated the sector), the number of banks and their market shares (a sector controlled by a few large banks is less competitive), and various aspects of the extent of development of financial markets (such as, how extensive are local or municipal securities markets). Another financial sector index—the fourth item in the list—measures how open a country is to flows of foreign capital. This is based on measuring the restrictions placed on financial transactions between residents and nonresidents.

Similarly, the real or nonfinancial sector indices measure the degree of deregulation and competition in trade, network industries, and labor markets. How open countries are to trade is measured with two indices; one looks at the tariffs imposed—higher tariffs translate into less openness to trade—while the other captures nontariff barriers such as restrictions on the use of proceeds from trade (e.g., surrender requirements) and licensing requirements for carrying out imports and exports. The network reforms index measures the extent of competition and deregulations in the electricity and telecommunications sectors—these are often considered to be sectors critical to the performance of other sectors of the economy.

For labor market reforms, we use an index that captures the extent of collective bargaining. This index tries to capture the view that higher levels of collective bargaining can hamper the performance of labor markets if they allow workers to enjoy salaries far above the value of what they produce.

One final index is intended to capture the impact of the overall institutional setting of a country on growth and inequality. This index assesses the impartiality of the legal system and the popular observance of the law. We interpret this index to capture the effect of broad legal reforms that potentially increase economic freedoms and the enforceability of property rights.

Each of these indicators has shortcomings as far as its ability to measure fully the competition and deregulation in that sector. For instance, competition in labor markets depends not just on collective bargaining but also on restrictions on hiring and firing, among other features. For the cross-country analysis of the type we are undertaking, however, these indices represent the best option available; and they are the very same data used by the IMF and other researchers in earlier studies of the growth effects of structural reforms.

Figure 4.2 plots the average level of the reform indicators by country group over time. All indicators take values between 0 and 1. Higher values of the index imply more liberalized economies. There has been a broad trend since the mid-1980s toward liberalizing domestic finance, trade, capital accounts, and network industries. The advanced economies have almost completely reformed along the domestic finance, trade, capital account, and law and order dimensions with almost all advanced countries having an index greater than 0.8. Low-income countries (LICs) and middle-income countries (MICs) lag behind advanced economies in these reform areas and the gap between advanced economies and MICs and LICs has been maintained through the years.

For network industries and labor market reforms, the picture is blurrier. For the collective bargaining index, there is no clear difference between advanced economies and MICs and LICs. In fact, there is large variation in the index within advanced economies, reflecting the fact that different advanced economies follow very different labor market models. Nordic countries, for example, have relatively high levels of collective bargaining (low values of the index) whereas Anglo-Saxon countries have low levels of collective bargaining (high values of the index). The average value of the index for MICs is actually higher than for advanced economies (MICs have less collective bargaining on average than advanced economies). Similarly, for network reforms, there is considerable overlap in the distribution of the index between advanced countries and the other two groups.

FIGURE 4.2: **Reform Indices Over Time by Income Level**

There has been a broad trend toward liberalizing domestic finance, trade, capital accounts
and network industries. Advanced economies have almost completely reformed along
the domestic finance, trade, capital account, and law and order dimensions. Middle- and
low-income countries continue to lag.

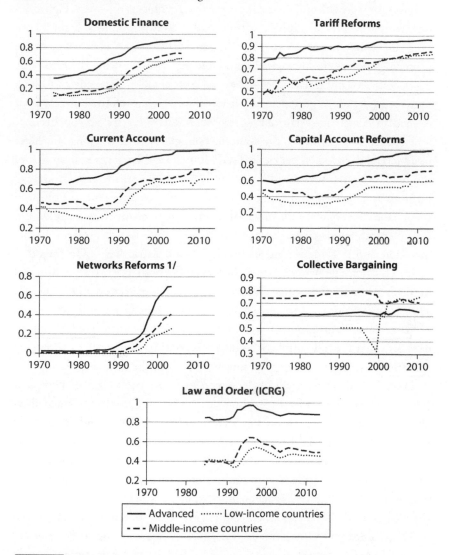

1/ Telecom and electricity

Note: All indices rescaled to lie between 0 and 1. Plots the average level of each reform index for each year
for the group of advanced countries, MICs, and LICs. Country coverage changes over time as more data
become available. Higher values indicate more liberalization.

Source: Ostry, Berg, and Kothari (2018).

EFFECTS OF STRUCTURAL REFORMS

We use standard statistical approaches (regression models) to assess the effect of reforms on growth and inequality—see the Technical Appendix. Figure 4.3 portrays our results in graphical form for all the reform indices. It shows the long-run change in per capita GDP (in percent) and the Gini coefficient (in percentage points) following structural reforms, thus showing the trade-offs between equity and efficiency that these reforms entail in the medium-to-long term. In this figure, we consider the impacts of moving the reform indicator from its median value to its seventy-fifth percentile value. What are our conclusions?

First, consider reforms to the domestic financial system. The long-run effect (over several decades) on per capita GDP of moving the reform indicator from the median to the seventy-fifth percentile would be an increase in average incomes by 25 percent and an increase in inequality by 2 percentage points. In theory, the effect of domestic financial reforms on inequality is ambiguous. On the one hand, reforms could reduce credit constraints, lead to greater financial inclusion, and thus reduce inequality (Galor and Zeira, 1993). On the other hand, if the rich have better access to the formal financial sector, further financial deepening could benefit them disproportionately (Greenwood and Jovanovic, 1990). Our empirical evidence suggests that the latter effect dominates.

Financial globalization (or capital account liberalization) confers output benefits when the full sample of countries is considered but comes with a big increase in inequality. We explore this more fully in the next chapter.

Lowering tariffs results in a long-run increase in per capita GDP of 15 percent (again over several decades)—consistent with the positive effect of trade liberalization on growth documented in Sachs and Warner (1995) and Frankel and Romer (1999)—without having a significant impact on inequality. However, with the other measure of trade liberalization—the current account liberalization index, which considers nontariff barriers—there is an impact not just on output but also an increase in inequality. An increase in the reform index from the median to the seventy-fifth percentile (Honduras or Trinidad and Tobago in 2005 compared to the United States) results in a long-run increase in per capita GDP of 12 percent and an increase in the Gini of 2.8 percentage points.

Network reforms do not appear to increase growth. But the effect of these reforms on growth differs markedly across countries and depends on the level of corruption, especially for the sample of LICs and MICs. It is likely that in

Structural reforms raise both long-run incomes and inequality, posing trade-offs between equity and efficiency.

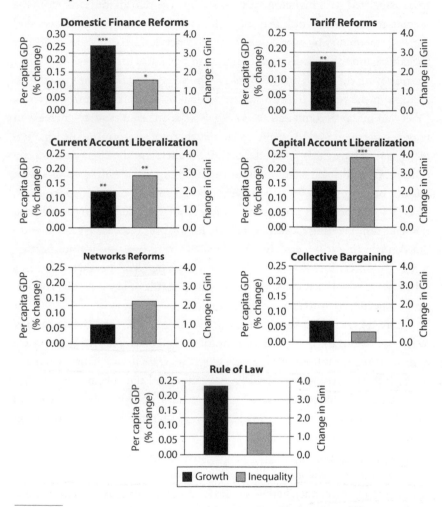

Note: Each panel plots the effect on the level of income and the level of inequality of moving the reform variable from the median to the seventy-fifth percentile. The first bar in each panel (and left scale) plots the percent change in per capita GDP over fifty years arising from a reform. The second column in every panel (and the right scale) plots the change in the Gini coefficient over fifty years arising from a similar reform episode. Statistical significance is indicated by asterisks above the bar: *** p < 0.01, ** p < 0.05, * p < 0.1

Source: Ostry, Berg, and Kothari (2018).

many countries with high levels of corruption, network reforms lead to the creation of monopolies in extractive industries that enrich some people in society but do not deliver broad gains in growth. Furthermore, network reforms seem to be associated with higher inequality. Moving the reform indicator from the median to the seventy-fifth percentile (India in 2005 compared to Australia) increases inequality by over 2 points. As with network reforms, the collective bargaining index has little impact on growth but raises inequality.

Improving the quality of the legal system is very beneficial for growth. An increase in the reform index from the median to the seventy-fifth percentile (Vietnam in 2005 compared to Portugal or Japan) results in an increase in long-run per capita GDP by 39 percent. Furthermore, reforming the legal system seems to have fairly small effects on inequality, and the effects are not significant. Overall, legal sector reforms thus seem to generate no trade-offs, with reforms being good for growth but at the same time not increasing inequality. These reforms probably improve the enforceability of property rights while at the same time creating a level playing field for all, thus increasing growth without contributing to adverse distributional effects. From a policy perspective, some caution is nonetheless warranted: ours is a de facto measure—that is, a subjective survey-based measure of perception of rule of law—and its connection to specific reforms is not obvious.

Figure 4.4 is a similar figure but restricted to our results for LICs and MICs. What stands out for this group of countries? Domestic finance reforms yield a smaller bang for output but lead to a bigger increase in inequality compared to the full set of countries. Tariff liberalization and the current account liberalization index continue to deliver somewhat different results: the use of the former generates more favorable outcomes than the latter; that is, higher income effects and lower inequality effects.

An important finding is that for this restricted sample of LICs and MICs there is no growth benefit from liberalizing capital account restrictions, but there is an increase in inequality. In these countries, moving the index from the median to the seventy-fifth percentile (Kenya or Philippines in 2005 compared to the United States) increases inequality by 2.6 points. The effect of external financial liberalization on growth depends crucially on the mix of capital flows (Blanchard, Ostry, Ghosh, and Chamon, 2016, 2017) and it is likely that the impact on inequality does as well. Foreign direct investment is more likely to boost growth, but can also increase inequality by raising skill premiums. Short-term debt flows,

Structural reforms in MICs and LICs also pose equity-efficiency trade-offs.

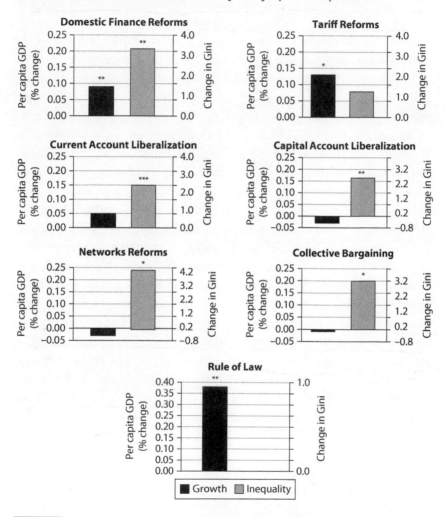

Note: Each panel plots the effect on the level of income and the level of inequality of moving the reform variable from the median to the seventy-fifth percentile. The left bar and scale in each panel plots the percent change in per capita GDP over fifty years arising from a reform. The right bar and scale in every panel plots the change in the Gini coefficient over fifty years arising from a similar reform episode. Statistical significance is indicated by asterisks above the bar: *** p<0.01, ** p<0.05, * p<0.1.

Source: Ostry, Berg, and Kothari (2018).

on the other hand, may increase the chances of sudden stops and financial crises, potentially harming growth on average while also perhaps raising inequality. Our empirical evidence shows that capital account liberalization poses a sharp trade-off between growth and equity, with such liberalization having weak effects on growth but leading to a strong increase in inequality.

There is some evidence of labor reforms increasing inequality in LICs and MICs. While less centralized systems may deliver more employment, they are likely to increase wage inequality, with the latter effect seemingly dominating in the macro data; reduced bargaining power of labor in a more decentralized system may also induce greater inequality.

To summarize, we find that many reforms increase inequality as well as growth. Our finding in chapter 3 that higher levels of inequality may reduce growth raises the question: What is the total effect of reforms on growth? That is, after considering the higher inequality following reforms, how much lower is the effect of reforms on growth (and is it even positive)? To answer this question, we carry out some simple calculations by combining results from the separate analyses of growth and inequality.

Figure 4.5 reports results for this calculation. In the case of domestic finance reforms, there is a large positive direct impact on average incomes; the dampening effect of inequality on growth only subtracts a little bit off the direct effect, leaving a sizable positive total effect. In the case of current account liberalization, the direct effect and the indirect effect almost cancel each other out. Capital account liberalization also has a positive total effect on average incomes for the full sample of countries; again, we stress that a similar calculation done for LICs and MICs would show a negative total effect as the direct effect on incomes is elusive while the impact on inequality is large.

EFFECTS OF STRUCTURAL REFORMS: COUNTRY CASES

The previous subsections present findings that many reforms raise both growth and inequality. The evidence is based on aggregating over the experience of several countries. Though we have used state-of-the-art techniques, it is nevertheless the case that econometric analysis cannot fully sort out the direction of causality nor can one be confident that the full set of factors influencing

FIGURE 4.5: Direct and Indirect Effect of Reforms on Level of Per Capita GDP

The total effect of reforms on incomes depends not only on the direct effect but on the extent to which the resulting increase in inequality subtracts from growth—the indirect effect.

– domestic

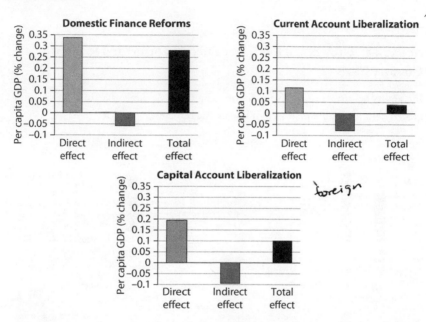

foreign

Note: Each panel plots the long-run direct effect, indirect effect (through increase in inequality), and total effect (sum of direct and indirect effects) of reforms on per capita GDP. In the growth regression, we include investment and education as controls. As market inequality is used as the dependent variable in the inequality regressions, we use market inequality as the control variable in the growth regressions when doing this exercise. This ensures consistency when combining the growth and inequality regression results.

Source: Ostry, Berg, and Kothari (2018).

growth and inequality is included in the regressions. Hence, it is useful to supplement the evidence with narrative histories of—and the political discourse surrounding—growth and inequality in particular countries.

To carry out this exercise, we grouped countries into three categories and then in each case picked two countries to analyze in detail: (1) countries where there was a broad-based reform effort in many areas—with Australia and Tanzania picked as case studies, (2) countries where there was a big push on domestic finance or trade—China and Indonesia, and (3) countries that have pushed ahead strongly on capital account liberalization or network reforms—Czech Republic and Argentina.

The reform dates are chosen based on combining information from the indices of structural reforms and the event studies. Figure 4.6 plots growth

FIGURE 4.6: **Growth and Inequality Effects of Structural Reforms, Country Cases**

Inequality before and after reforms for our country cases shows that, in most cases, both growth and inequality increased following the reforms.

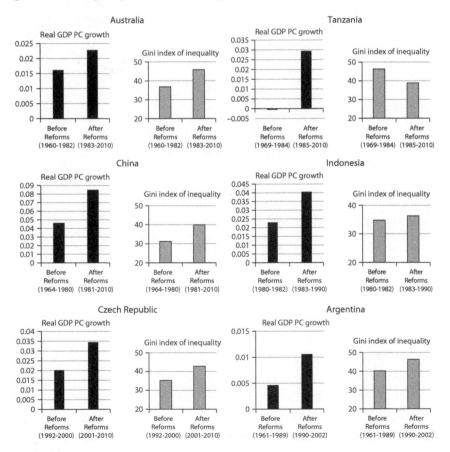

Source: Ostry, Berg, and Kothari (2018).

and inequality before and after the reforms for our country cases showing that, in most cases, both growth and inequality increased following the reforms. The growth impact from reforms has been studied extensively by other authors. What we see is that there was also an increase in inequality in the aftermath of reforms, as suggested by our panel regressions and event studies. We next discuss whether the narrative evidence gives a sense of the mechanisms discussed in the literature review.

Broad-Based Reforms

Australia: In the 1980s and 1990s, Australia implemented extensive domestic financial sector reforms, including removing interest rate controls and some bank lending restrictions, and taking steps to foster increased competition. There was also comprehensive trade liberalization from the late 1980s through the 1990s, including phased reductions in tariffs across sectors. Collective bargaining systems were overhauled to introduce more labor market flexibility. There was also a major domestic finance reform in 1991 and network reform in 1996.

That Australia experienced a growth payoff from these reforms is widely accepted: the country has enjoyed steady growth over the past two decades. Adhikari, Duval, Hu, and Loungani (2018) show that Australia's post-reform output performance has been better than that of a peer group of countries that did not undertake similar reforms. What is noteworthy is that market inequality has also increased following this period of reform: market Gini rose from 42 in 1991 to 47 in 2005. Concerns about these distributional effects have been part of the political discourse in Australia (Conley 2004), but were muted by the strong growth performance and by extensive redistributive policies (Greenville et al. 2013).

Tanzania: The country has launched two major waves of reforms. The Economic Recovery Program in 1986 focused on trade and exchange rate liberalization and a second effort in the mid-1990s focused on financial and labor market reforms and on privatization. Reforms paid off in higher growth: Tanzania's per capita GDP growth averaged almost 3 percent a year over the period 1985–2010, substantially higher than its past growth and higher than that of its peers.

However, contrary to the experience of many other countries that have conducted broad-based reforms, inequality declined over the period. The country's success in diversifying into labor-intensive manufacturing is often mentioned as a possible reason, but a full explanation of the country's favorable distributional outcomes is still being debated (Atkinson and Lugo 2014). There is also some concern about more recent distributional developments: Treichel (2005) notes that, despite strong macroeconomic performance between 2001 and 2007, "social and poverty indicators for the country as a whole have not improved substantially over the past decade," with progress on these indicators limited to the commercial capital, Dar es Salaam.

In general, countries carrying out broad-based reforms have seen increases in both growth and inequality. Examples include India (following reform in the mid-1990s), Uganda (1990–1995), Costa Rica (1990s), Ghana (late 1980s), Mozambique (mid-1990s), and Rwanda (early 1990s).

Trade-Focused and/or Domestic Finance-Focused Reforms

China: Starting in the late 1980s, China embarked on trade liberalization and domestic financial sector reforms. The network reforms and opening up of the capital account came much later, in the 2000s. Our empirical evidence would suggest a large growth impact initially from the trade and financial sector reforms, perhaps with some moderation as the growth impact of the later reforms is muted according to our evidence; inequality should increase, with the impact likely rising over time as the later reforms have stronger distributional consequences. As is well known, China has enjoyed remarkable growth following the launch of its reforms and this has enabled the rescue of millions from abject poverty. At the same time, inequality has increased dramatically, with large rural-urban income differentials and divergence between coastal and interior provinces (Yang 1999; Tsui 1996). Our evidence suggests that as capital account liberalization proceeds, such distributional impacts will grow and steps will be needed, through redistribution and other means, to contain their adverse impacts, including on growth itself. Many other countries in Asia that have followed a similar export-oriented strategy have experienced a similar increase in inequality in recent decades.

Indonesia: Faced with declining oil revenues and balance-of-payments problems, the Indonesian government moved toward greater market orientation. The financial system was deregulated in two stages, with abolition of most bank lending controls, and the abolition of ceilings on deposit rates at state banks in 1983 and changes in controls to bank borrowing and lending rates and a relaxation of banking entry norms in 1988. "The combination of the June 1983 and October 1988 packages took Indonesia's banking system in just five years from state bank dominance and bureaucratic suffocation to being an effervescent, private sector-driven collection of institutions, remarkably free of government intervention," according to McLeod (1994). Reforms led to increased financial deepening, with private sector credit as a percent of GDP increasing from about 10 percent in 1980 to almost 50 percent in 1990. However, progress on financial inclusion was a lot slower, and Indonesia continues to lag behind Asian peers on the inclusion dimension. Growth picked up in the aftermath of the reforms, so much so that Indonesia was hailed as a miracle performer in the decade between the 1988 reforms and the start of the Asian crisis. Over the same period, however, inequality increased, as described by Jayadev (2005): "In the new regime, rapid urban growth (financed by abundant credit) changed employment patterns by moving people from unpaid family labor and the agricultural sector toward urban centers and cities. At the same time, sectors which had provided employment for low skilled workers declined," exacerbating wage differentials.

A Thrust Toward Open Capital Markets and/or Network Reforms

Czech Republic: Among the transition economies, the Czech Republic was a "pioneer . . . in achieving a high degree of liberalization of its capital account relatively early in the transition process" (Arvai 2005). Liberalization of inflows was faster than the removal of outflow restrictions. FDI was the first major item to be liberalized in the early 1990s; most capital transactions were de jure liberalized by September 1995; and the Organization for Economic Cooperation and Development (OECD) accession took place in December 1995. Growth and inequality increased as they did in other transition economies, but some observers note that the Czech Republic underperformed on growth and suffered worse distributional outcomes than other transition economies because it focused excessively on promarket reforms such as opening of the capital account but "grossly neglected the need to establish a functioning legal framework and corporate governance of firms and banks" (Svejnar 2002). In the Czech Republic, the Gini coefficient in the 2000s was 7.5 points higher than in the 1990s, three times more on average than for other Central European transition economies.

proof for current then capital

Argentina: In 1990, the country privatized the state-owned telecommunications company. This had an immediate macroeconomic impact due to massive job cuts, particularly affecting the least-skilled workers, who generally were unable to find new jobs. Though rates gradually fell after privatization, they fell much more quickly in the commercial and long-distance segments most used by the wealthy than in the local tariffs most heavily used by the poor (Galperin 2005). This case is typical of many in the developing world, particularly in Latin America: the end of state monopolies in transportation and telecommunications contributes to income inequality as a result of substantial job loss of low-skilled workers, price increases, and a decline in real output, but with substantial benefits for the powerful and wealthy (Auriol 2005; McKenzie and Mookherjee 2003). Though many factors contribute to high inequality in many Latin American countries, network reforms are considered to have played an important role.

DESIGNING STRUCTURAL REFORMS

As noted in the introduction to the book, economists have traditionally paid attention to the efficiency gains of policies but ignored their equity impacts. Our results suggest that, on average, measurable and significant distributional impacts have been associated with structural reforms. We call attention to this fact not to argue that policymakers should shy away from pursuing reform. On the contrary, our results show that many reforms have a positive impact on growth even taking into account the effects on inequality. Rather, we lend weight to the call for reforms that are designed with distributional consequences in mind.

Our results also suggest that the growth impact of reforms cannot always be taken for granted. The consensus policies of free markets, macroeconomic discipline, and globalization have broadly worked, but this does not mean that departures from them are bound to be costly. In fact, with the passage of time, how strictly Chile adhered to consensus policies is being reassessed. Many have come around to the view expressed by Joseph Stiglitz that Chile "is an example of a success of combining markets with appropriate regulation" (2002 interview). Stiglitz notes, in particular, that in the early years of

↳ case by case

its move to neoliberalism, Chile imposed "controls on the inflows of capital, so they wouldn't be inundated in the way that Thailand was, which led to the [1997–98 Asian] crisis." In later years, with its economy and its financial markets much more developed, Chile saw fit to lift these capital controls. Chile's experience, and that of other countries, suggests that no fixed agenda delivers good outcomes for all countries for all times.

CHAPTER 5

FINANCIAL GLOBALIZATION AND INEQUALITY

I n June 1979, shortly after winning a landmark election, Margaret Thatcher carried out what her supporters regarded as "one of her best and most revolutionary acts" (Heath, *The Telegraph*, 2015) and her critics deplored as starting a global trend whose "downside . . . proved to be painful" (Schiffrin 2016).

What were these actions? Thatcher eliminated restrictions on "the ability to move money in and out" of the United Kingdom. The *Telegraph* wrote that "in the economic dark ages that were the 1970s" UK citizens could "forget about buying a property abroad, purchasing foreign equities or financing a holiday . . . The economic impact was devastating: companies were reluctant to invest in the UK as it was tough even for them to move money back to their home countries." Thatcher abolished "all of these nonsensical rules and liberalized the UK's capital account." Thatcher's move toward financial openness was followed by Germany in 1984 and by other European countries and many emerging market economies in Latin America and Asia over the coming decade.

At its annual meeting in October 1997 in Hong Kong SAR, the IMF put forth its arguments for why countries should keep moving toward full capital account liberalization, the elimination of restrictions on the movement of funds into and out of a country. The IMF's then–First Deputy Managing Director Stanley Fischer called liberalization "an inevitable step on the path of development which cannot be avoided and should be embraced." Fischer noted that liberalization ensures that "residents and governments are able to borrow and lend on favorable terms, and domestic financial markets become more efficient as a result of the introduction of advanced financial technologies, leading to better allocation of both saving and investment" (Fischer 1997). While acknowledging that liberalization "increases the vulnerability of the economy to swings in [market] sentiment," Fischer argued that the potential benefits of opening up the capital account outweigh the costs. As Maurice Obstfeld—the IMF's former chief economist since 2015—also noted at the time, "economic theory leaves no doubt about the potential advantages" of capital account liberalization (Obstfeld 1998).

But financial globalization also had its critics. Harvard University economist Dani Rodrik argued at the time that the evidence on the benefits of capital account liberalization was elusive, while the costs in terms of increased risk of crises were high. He warned that letting capital flow freely across the world would leave economies "hostage to the whims and fancies of two dozen or so thirty-somethings in London, Frankfurt and New York. A finance minister whose top priority is to keep foreign investors happy will pay less attention to developmental goals" (Rodrik 1998). Even some proponents of capital account liberalization, such as Obstfeld, warned that "this duality of benefits and risks is inescapable in the real world."

The evidence over the past few decades has proved such views prescient. The benefits of liberalization in terms of increased investment and growth have continued to be difficult to establish, while there are numerous cases of liberalization leading to economic volatility and financial crisis. This in turn has adverse consequences for many in the economy, particularly for those who are not well off. Since 1980, there have been about 150 episodes of surges in capital inflows in more than 50 emerging market economies; about 20 percent of the time, these episodes end in a financial crisis, and many of these crises are associated with large output declines (Ghosh, Ostry, and Qureshi 2016).

Our work adds an additional cost: the impact on equity. Liberalization affects the relative bargaining power of companies and workers (that is, of capital and labor, respectively, in the jargon of economists) because capital is generally able to move across national boundaries with greater ease than labor. The threat of being able to move production abroad can lower labor's bargaining power and thus the share of the income pie that goes to workers.

↳ capital is mobile, labor is stuck

MEASURING FINANCIAL GLOBALIZATION

The restrictions that countries place on various cross-border financial trans-actions have been tabulated by the IMF since the 1950s. Using these reports, Chinn and Ito (2006) have constructed a measure that adds up how many restrictions have been in place in different countries and how these restrictions have been relaxed or tightened over the years. The index is available for 182 countries, in many but not all cases from 1970 to 2010, and it ranges from −2 (more restricted capital account) to 2.5 (less restricted). The score of the capital account openness index varies greatly across income groups, with higher restrictions typically recorded in low-income countries (LICs) and lower-middle-income countries (LMICs).

Not every change in this index is likely to represent a deliberate and major policy action, like that of Thatcher's, to liberalize the capital account. And while Thatcher's action drew attention at the time, actions by other govern-ments can be difficult to track. We thus try to infer the timing of major pol-icy changes by using large changes in the index. Specifically, we assume that a financial openness episode takes place when the annual change in the indicator exceeds by two standard deviations the average annual change over all observa-tions in our dataset (i.e., exceeds 0.76). This criterion identifies 224 episodes of liberalization, with the majority of them occurring during the last two decades (figure 5.1). The largest number of episodes has occurred during the 1990s and among middle-income countries (MICs).

EFFECTS OF FINANCIAL GLOBALIZATION

What happens to output and inequality after an episode of financial global-ization? Output growth in the years preceding an episode averages just short of 4 percent, as shown in figure 5.2. It gets a very short-lived boost in the year following an episode (to 4 percent), but that has subsided five years after the episode. Inequality increases, with the Gini rising from about 44 to nearly 45.5 within five years after an episode.

We now subject these results to more formal tests. Figure 5.3 tracks what hap-pens to output and inequality following an episode of financial openness. It reports the estimated effect of liberalization, with the dotted lines showing the bounds

Number of Capital Account Liberalization Episodes

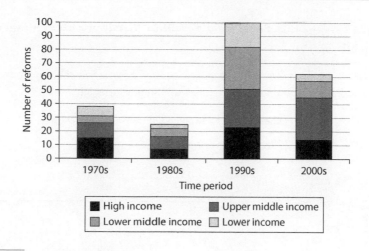

Source: Furceri, Loungani, and Ostry (2018).

FIGURE 5.2: Growth and Inequality Before and After Capital Account Liberalizations

Output gains are small and short-lived whereas inequality increases persistently after capital account liberalization.

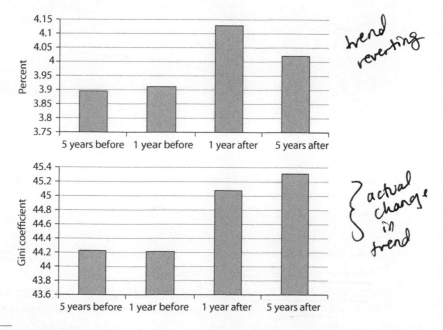

Source: Furceri and Loungani (2017).

FIGURE 5.3: The Effect of Capital Account Liberalization on Output and Inequality

Capital account liberalization reforms have not had a significant effect on output, but have had significant and long-lasting effects on income inequality.

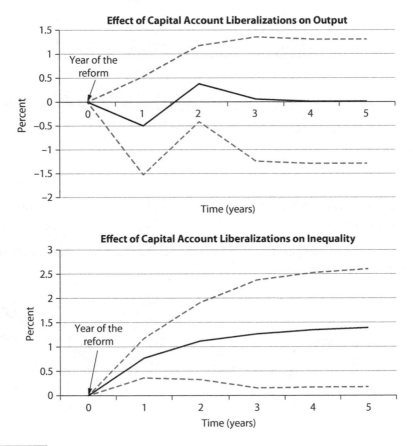

Note: The solid line corresponds to the estimated effect (the so-called impulse-response function—IRF); dotted lines correspond to 90 percent confidence bands.

Source: Furceri, Loungani, and Ostry (2018).

within which the true effect might lie. The results suggest that capital account liberalization episodes have not had a significant effect on output (any boost is again quite short-lived). However, they have had significant and long-lasting effects on income inequality: following a capital account liberalization episode, the Gini index increases by about 0.8 percent in the very short term—one year after the occurrence of the reform episode—and by about 1.4 percent in the medium term—five years after the occurrence of the reform episode.

These effects are quantitatively significant. Gini coefficients change slowly over time as previously noted. Changes in the Gini have a standard deviation of 2 percent (that is, nearly 70 percent of the time, when the Gini index changes, it does so by less than 2 percent). The effects shown in figure 5.3 are therefore quite large relative to the standard deviation; simply put, episodes of capital account liberalization lead to big increases in inequality. Figure 5.4 shows that shares of incomes going to the top 1 percent, top 5 percent, and top 10 percent all increase following capital account liberalization reforms.

In the textbook model of perfect competition, each factor of production—capital and labor—gets its just rewards based on its contribution to a company's profits. But a more realistic description of the world is one of imperfect competition, where the division of the economic pie is influenced by the relative bargaining power of capital and labor. In his 1997 book, *Has Globalization Gone Too Far?*, Rodrik argued that capital account liberalization tilts the playing field in favor of capital, the more mobile of the factors of production. Jayadev (2007) argued similarly that "the imminent and plausible threat" by capital that it will relocate abroad causes workers to lose bargaining power and some of their share of income.

Our results, presented in the top panel of Figure 5.5, are indeed consistent with this conjecture: capital account liberalization episodes have significant and long-lasting effects on the labor share of income. In particular, the estimates suggest that reforms have typically decreased the labor share of income by about 0.6 percentage point in the short term—one year after the reform—and by about 0.8 percentage point in the medium term—five years after the reform.

As was the case with the Gini measure of inequality, these are big effects. The changes in the labor share have a standard deviation of 2.25 percentage points (that is, nearly 70 percent of the time, when the labor share changes, it does so by less than 2.25 percentage points). Hence, capital account liberalization is associated with large declines in labor shares.

As we noted in chapter 4, the direction of causality is difficult to sort out using econometric analysis. In that chapter we therefore used the narrative histories of specific countries to complement the econometric analysis. Here we use another technique to bolster confidence that it is indeed the policy action that leads to inequality and not inequality that leads to the policy actions. This technique involves the use of industry-level (sectoral) data instead of economy-wide (aggregate) measures of inequality. The idea is that it is quite unlikely

Capital account liberalization increases the shares of income owned by the top 1 percent,
top 5 percent, and top 10 percent.

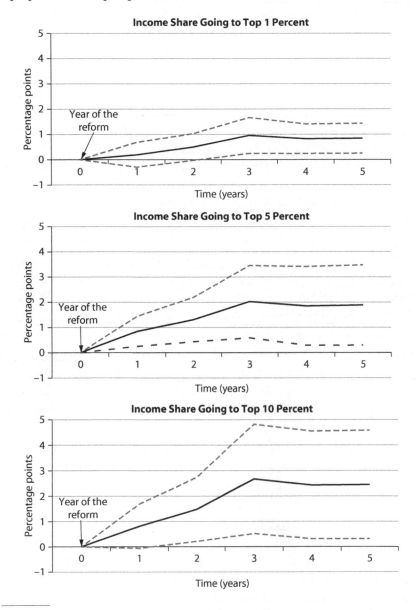

Note: The solid line corresponds to the estimated effect (the so-called impulse-response function—IRF);
dotted lines correspond to 90 percent confidence bands. The x-axis denotes time. t = 0 is the year of the reform.

Source: Furceri, Loungani, and Ostry (2018).

Capital account liberalization reforms leads to long-lasting declines in the labor share of income.

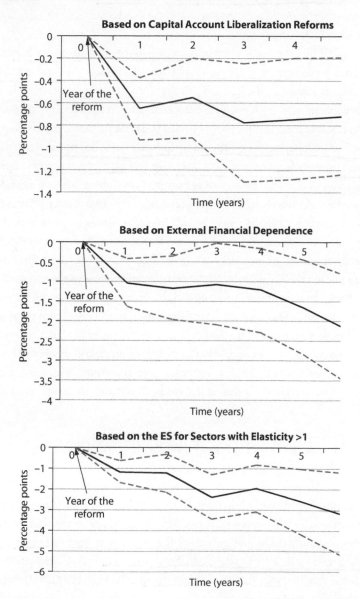

Note: The solid line corresponds to the estimated effect (the so-called impulse-response function—IRF); dotted lines correspond to 90 percent confidence bands. The x-axis denotes time. t = 0 is the year of the reform.

Source: Furceri, Loungani, and Ostry (2018).

that capital account liberalization would be undertaken by governments due to changes in inequality in a particular sector of the economy. As shown in the middle panel of figure 5.5, opening up the capital account leads to a decline in industry labor shares as well.

We also find that the decline in labor shares is higher in industries where capital (e.g., machines) can be more easily substituted for labor in the production process. This is shown in the bottom panel of figure 5.5. In contrast, in industries where machines cannot easily do the job of labor, we find that there is little change in labor shares. This pattern of findings has an intuitive explanation: in industries where labor can be more easily dispensed with, it is more likely to lose bargaining power when the economy opens up to free flows of foreign capital.

The impact of the loss of bargaining power may be more severe for workers in advanced economies than in emerging economies for two reasons. First, companies in advanced economies may be in a better position to make a credible threat to relocate abroad—where wages are lower. Second, in many emerging market economies capital is scarce relative to labor. The arrival of foreign investment capital can raise the demand for labor, mitigating some of the effects of the relative change in bargaining power due to the opening of the capital account.

The impact of capital account liberalization on inequality holds even after several other determinants of inequality—such as openness to trade; changes in the size of government; and regulation of product, labor, and credit markets—are accounted for. Using alternate measures of capital account liberalization provided by other researchers (Quinn and Toyoda 2008) also gives similar results.

EFFECTS OF FINANCIAL GLOBALIZATION: CHANNELS

What accounts for the weak impact of liberalization on output and the strong effects on inequality? We investigate two key channels conjectured in previous work. First, opening up to foreign capital flows can be a source of volatility—with large capital inflows followed by outflows and vice versa. Critics of liberalization insist that this volatility is a source of crisis. Rodrik (1998), for instance, argued that the sudden outflow of foreign capital from Asian economies in 1997 left them "mired in a severe economic crisis." Rodrik notes that this is not an "isolated incident" and that "boom-and-bust cycles are hardly a sideshow or a minor blemish in international capital flows; they are the main story."

Second, while liberalization should expand the access of domestic borrowers to sources of capital, the strength of domestic financial institutions plays a crucial role in the extent to which this takes place. In many countries, financial institutions do not offer a wide range of services and large numbers of people, particularly the poor, do not have access to credit. Such economies are described as having low financial depth—the amount of credit extended is low relative to the size of the economy. Under these circumstances, liberalization may improve financial access mostly of those well-off, which could dampen the output effects while exacerbating the impact on inequality.

 We find evidence in favor of both channels: the adverse impact of liberalization on output and inequality is greater when it is followed by a crisis and where financial depth and inclusion are low. To study the first channel, we separated cases in which capital account liberalizations were followed by a financial crisis from cases in which no crisis ensued. The impact of openness on inequality differs markedly between the two cases, as shown in figure 5.6. In particular, when there was a crisis, there was a decline in output of 5 percent and an increase in inequality of 3.5 percent; in contrast, in the absence of a crisis, output increased a bit and there was a smaller increase in inequality.

The effect of liberalization on inequality also differs by financial depth and inclusiveness. We separate countries where financial markets are not very deep from others using an indicator compiled by the Fraser Institute. In countries with high financial depth, output increases and inequality falls; in countries with low financial depth, output falls by 3 percent and inequality goes up by 2.5 percent. Similarly, in countries with low financial inclusion—where very few have access to bank accounts and financial services—liberalization has little impact on output but leads to a sharp increase in inequality.

POLICY IMPLICATIONS FOR LOW-INCOME COUNTRIES

Rising income inequality within countries has received renewed attention in recent years. Much of the focus has been on advanced and emerging economies; however, many LICs also experienced growing income inequality from the late 1980s to the early 2000s and again more recently. Some observers have pointed out that these periods of rising inequality coincide with increasing openness to foreign capital in these countries (Goldin and Reinert 2012). In comparison to other country groups, LICs currently have greater restrictions on the capital account, and thus have more space to relax such restrictions in years to come. Thus, understanding the consequences of further opening up the capital account is likely to remain in the near future an important policy issue for LICs. In this set of countries, as in the full sample, episodes of capital account liberalization have been followed by increases in inequality, which have been particularly sharp in some countries such as Egypt (figure 5.7).

When deciding to liberalize the capital account following the footsteps of high-income countries (HICs), policymakers in LICs should take into consideration these distributional effects and ensure that the supporting conditions are in place so that all segments of society can reap the benefits of opening up. This warrants special attention because, in general, most of these countries have weak financial institutions and access to credit markets is quite limited. More than half of the poorest 40 percent of the population in developing countries are without access to formal banking accounts. Therefore, liberalizing the capital account may exacerbate the bias in accessing financial products in favor of those who are already well-off. Indeed, we find that even within this group of countries, the impact of financial openness on inequality is particularly strong where the extent of development of financial markets and financial inclusion is limited (figure 5.8).

FIGURE 5.6: The Effect of Capital Account Liberalization on Output and Inequality

The adverse impact of liberalization on output and inequality is greater when it is followed by a crisis and where financial depth and inclusion are low.

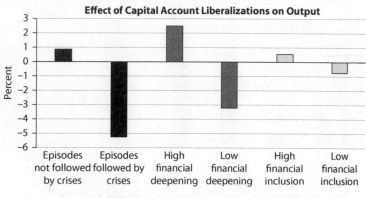

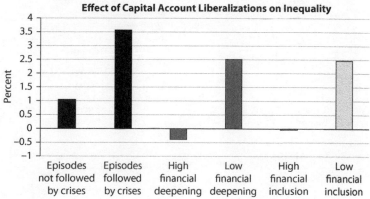

Source: Furceri, Loungani, and Ostry (2018).

FIGURE 5.7: Evolution of Gini Before and After Capital Account Liberalization

In low-income countries, capital account liberalization increases income inequality. The long-lasting increases can be observed in countries such as Egypt, Nepal, Uganda, and Bolivia.

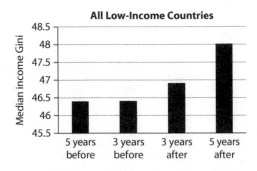

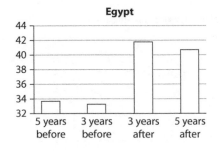

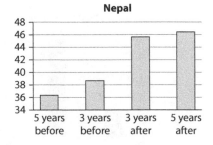

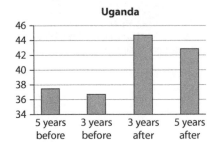

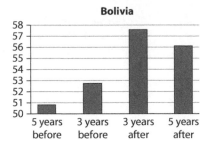

Source: Furceri, Ge, and Loungani (2016).

FIGURE 5.8: Effect of Capital Account Liberalization on Inequality in Low-Income Countries

Even within the group of low-income countries, financial liberalization leads to a stronger increase in inequality where the extent of development of financial markets and financial inclusion is limited.

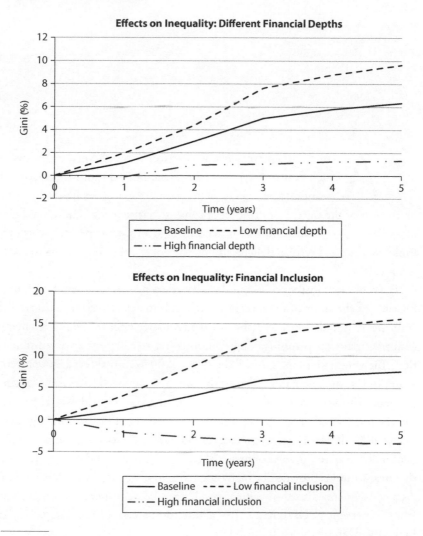

Source: Furceri, Ge, and Loungani (2016).

CHAPTER 6

AUSTERITY AND INEQUALITY

A long with increased competition through various means—such as opening up to foreign capital—an important part of economic policies over the past three decades has been curbs on the size of the state. Privatization of some government functions has been one way to achieve this. Another is to control government spending through limits on the size on fiscal deficits and on the ability of governments to accumulate debt.

The economic history of recent decades offers many examples of such limits, such as the limit of 60 percent on the public-debt-to-GDP ratio set for countries to join the euro area (the so-called Maastricht criteria); this led many countries that were planning to join the euro area to carry out fiscal consolidation. The aftermath of the Great Recession of 2007–2009 offers a more recent example. On the one hand, it led to the most pronounced increase in unemployment the advanced countries had seen in the post–World War II period. On the other hand, it led to a significant increase in public debt, in large part due to the collapse in tax revenues as incomes fell. Other contributors to the debt buildup were the costs of financial bailouts of banks and companies, and the fiscal stimulus provided by many countries to stave off a Great Depression. As a consequence, in advanced economies public debt increased on average from 70 percent of GDP in 2007 to about 100 percent of GDP in 2011—its highest level in fifty years (Ghosh et al. 2013).

Against this backdrop, many governments started to undertake policies to reduce debt through a combination of spending cuts and tax increases. When former British Prime Minister David Cameron announced his government's deficit-reduction plans in 2011, he said: "Those who argue that dealing with our deficit and promoting growth are somehow alternatives are wrong. You cannot put off the first in order to promote the second" (Cameron 2011).

Is there a case for countries in a situation similar to the United Kingdom's in 2011 to pay down the public debt quickly? Two arguments are usually made in support of doing so in countries with ample fiscal space—that is, countries where there is little real prospect of a fiscal crisis. The first is that, while large adverse shocks occur rarely (the Great Depression of the 1930s and the Global Financial Crisis in more recent times), when they do occur, it is helpful to have used the quiet times to pay down the debt. The second argument is that high debt is bad for growth (because more distortive taxation is required to service a higher level of debt)—and, therefore, to lay a firm foundation for growth, paying down the debt is essential.

It is surely the case that many countries (e.g., in Southern Europe in the 2010s) have had little choice but to engage in fiscal consolidation, because developments in financial markets—the increase in their sovereign spreads (the interest rates their governments would have to pay to borrow) did not leave them the space to continue borrowing (Ghosh, Ostry, and Qureshi 2013). But the need for consolidation in some countries does not translate to all countries. Markets generally attach very low probabilities of a debt crisis in countries that have a strong track record of being fiscally responsible (Mendoza and Ostry 2008). That track record gives them latitude not to raise taxes or cut productive spending in a position of high debt, if the costs of austerity outweigh the benefits. And for countries with a strong track record, the benefit, in terms of the insurance against a future fiscal crisis, turns out to be remarkably small, even at very high debt ratios. For example, moving from a debt ratio of 120 percent of GDP to 100 percent of GDP over a few years buys very little in terms of reduced crisis risk—the probability of a crisis does not fall very much even when debt is reduced from such high levels (Baldacci et al. 2011).

But even if the insurance benefit is small, it may still be worth acquiring if the cost is sufficiently small. It turns out, however, that the cost is actually large—much larger than the benefit. The reason is the costs of the tax increases or expenditure cuts needed to bring down the debt are much larger than the reduced crisis risk from lower debt (see Ostry, Ghosh, and Espinoza 2015, for the economic model that demonstrates this point). Faced with a choice between living with the higher debt—and allowing the debt ratio to decline organically through economically growth—or deliberately running budgetary surpluses to reduce the debt, governments with ample fiscal space will do better by living with the debt.

MEASURING FISCAL CONSOLIDATION

Countries have not often heeded this advice. To the contrary, worries about the debt level have prompted numerous episodes of austerity by advanced economies over the past three decades. We show that such episodes have lowered incomes and raised unemployment over the short run to the medium run (over three to five years). Past austerity has also increased the Gini measure of inequality significantly, lowered the share of the income going to labor, and had a particularly strong impact on the long-term unemployment rate.

The measure of fiscal consolidation used in this chapter is based on previous IMF research (DeVries et al. 2011). This measure focuses on *policy* actions—tax hikes or spending cuts—taken by governments with the intent of reducing the budget deficit. This may seem to be the obvious thing to do but it is not the way fiscal consolidation has been measured in previous studies.

Typically, in the past, fiscal consolidation has been measured by successful budget *outcomes*. Specifically, the cyclically adjusted primary balance—the government's primary balance adjusted for the estimated effects of business cycle fluctuations—is used as a measure of fiscal consolidation. The cyclical adjustment is needed because tax revenue and government spending move automatically with the business cycle. The hope is that, after this cyclical adjustment, changes in fiscal variables reflect policymakers' decisions to change tax rates and spending levels. An increase in the cyclically adjusted budget balance would therefore, in principle, reflect a deliberate policy decision to cut the deficit.

In practice, however, budget outcomes turn out to be an imperfect measure of policy intent. One problem is that the cyclical adjustment suffers from measurement errors. In particular, it fails to remove swings in government tax revenue associated with asset price or commodity price movements from the fiscal data, resulting in changes in the balance that are not necessarily linked to actual policy changes. For example, in Ireland in 2009, the collapse in stock and housing prices induced a sharp reduction in the budget balance despite the implementation of tax hikes and spending cuts exceeding 4.5 percent of GDP.

Another problem is that the standard approach ignores the motivation behind fiscal actions. Thus, it includes years in which governments deliberately tightened policy to restrain excessive domestic demand. For example, in Finland in 2000, there was an asset price boom and rapid growth, and the government decided to cut spending to reduce the risk of economic overheating. If a fiscal tightening is a *response to* domestic demand pressures, it is not valid for estimating the short-term effects of fiscal policy on economic activity, even if it is associated with a sharp rise in the budget balance.

For these reasons, we measure fiscal consolidation based on policy actions. This gives us 173 episodes of consolidation for 17 OECD economies from 1978 to 2009. The magnitude of the consolidation during an episode is about 1 percent of GDP on average.

THE EFFECTS OF AUSTERITY

Using this more accurate measure of austerity, the evidence from the past is clear: fiscal consolidations typically have the short-run effect of reducing incomes and raising unemployment. A fiscal consolidation of 1 percent of GDP reduces inflation-adjusted incomes by about 0.6 percent and raises the unemployment rate by almost 0.5 percentage point (figure 6.1) within two years, with some recovery thereafter.

The reduction in incomes from fiscal consolidations is even larger if central banks do not or cannot blunt some of the pain through a monetary policy stimulus. The fall in interest rates associated with monetary stimulus supports investment and consumption, and the concomitant depreciation of the currency boosts net exports. Ireland in 1987 and Finland and Italy in 1992 are examples of countries that undertook fiscal consolidations but where large devaluations of the currency helped provide a boost to net exports.

Unfortunately, these pain relievers are not easy to come by in today's environment. In many economies, central banks can provide only a limited monetary stimulus because policy interest rates are already near zero. Moreover, if many countries carry out fiscal austerity at the same time, the reduction in

FIGURE 6.1: Effect of Fiscal Consolidation on Income and Unemployment

Fiscal consolidation reduces incomes and raises unemployment in the short run.

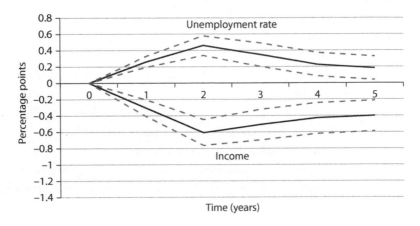

Note: Impact of 1 percent of GDP fiscal consolidation on GDP and unemployment.

Source: Ball, Leigh, and Loungani (2011).

incomes in each country is likely to be greater, because not all countries can reduce the value of their currency and increase net exports simultaneously.

What about the impact on inequality? As we did in the case of capital account liberalization in chapter 5, it is useful to look at a before-and-after plot of the data before proceeding to more formal tests. This is done in figure 6.2, which shows how the Gini coefficient was evolving, on average, before an episode of fiscal consolidation and how the path changed after consolidation. The path of the Gini coefficient clearly changes at the onset of austerity. Eight years after the start of an episode, the Gini coefficient is 1.5 percent points higher than its original value.

This suggestive evidence is corroborated by formal econometric methods, the results of which are shown in figure 6.3. The figure shows the estimated effect of fiscal consolidation on the Gini coefficient and the associated confidence bands (dotted lines). It is evident that consolidation has a long-lasting effect on income inequality. In particular, the estimates suggest that consolidation episodes have increased the Gini index by about 0.1 percentage point

FIGURE 6.2: Inequality Before and After Fiscal Consolidation

Fiscal consolidation tends to have long-lasting negative impacts on income inequality.

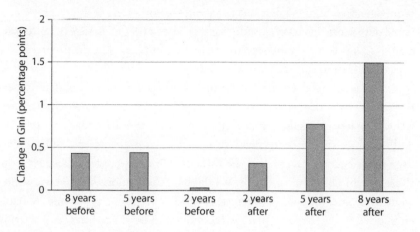

Note: The y-axis shows the percentage point change in the Gini coefficient.

Source: Ball, Furceri, Leigh, and Loungani (2013).

FIGURE 6.3: Effect of Fiscal Consolidation on Inequality

Fiscal consolidations are associated with significant and persistent increases in income inequality.

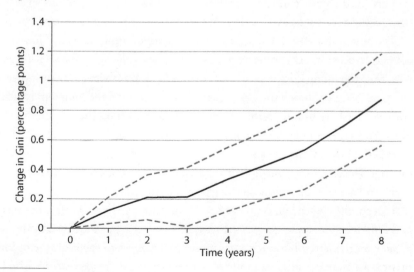

Note: The dotted lines show one standard error band.

Source: Ball, Furceri, Leigh, and Loungani (2013).

(equivalent to about 0.4 percent) in the short term—one year after the occurrence of the consolidation episode—and by about 0.9 percentage point (equivalent to 3.4 percent) in the medium term—eight years after the occurrence of the consolidation episode.

Another way to assess the distributional effects of fiscal consolidation measures is to look at their effect on different types of income. As noted in chapter 2, a traditional way of splitting total income is into the share that goes to labor and the share that goes to capital in the form of profits, rents, and the like. This harks back to times when the roles of workers were fairly distinct from those of capitalists and landlords. While these distinctions have eroded somewhat over time, the split between wages and other forms of income "remains embedded in our national income accounts and in our politics" as a starting point for describing how income is divided between Main Street and Wall Street (Galbraith 2016).

The pain of consolidation is not borne equally. Fiscal consolidation reduces the slice of the pie going to wage earners. For every 1 percent of GDP of fiscal consolidation, inflation-adjusted wage income typically shrinks by 0.9 percent, while inflation-adjusted profit and rents fall by only 0.3 percent. Also, while the decline in wage income persists over time, the decline in profits and rents is short-lived (figure 6.4, top two panels). As a consequence, labor's share of the income pie shrinks as a result of consolidation (figure 6.4, bottom panel).

The reasons for wage income declining more than profits and rents have not yet been studied much. Some fiscal austerity plans call for public sector wage cuts, thus providing a direct channel for this effect. But there could be indirect channels as well, through the impact of consolidations on total unemployment and on the share of long-term unemployed in the total. Though the unemployed do receive unemployment benefits, their incomes nevertheless take a substantial hit and thus are an important source of the decline in overall wage income. The long-term unemployed, particularly, run out of benefits at some point and are thus likely to suffer sharp falls in income.

Indeed, the evidence shows that fiscal consolidations raise both short-term and long-term unemployment, as shown in figure 6.5, but the impact is much greater on the latter. Long-term unemployment refers to spells of unemployment lasting greater than six months. Moreover, within three years the rise in short-term unemployment due to fiscal consolidation comes to an end, but long-term unemployment remains higher even after five years.

FIGURE 6.4: Effect of Fiscal Consolidation on Labor's Share of Income

Decline in wage income persists over time after fiscal consolidation whereas the decline in profits and rents is short. Therefore, labor's share of the income shrinks as a result of consolidation.

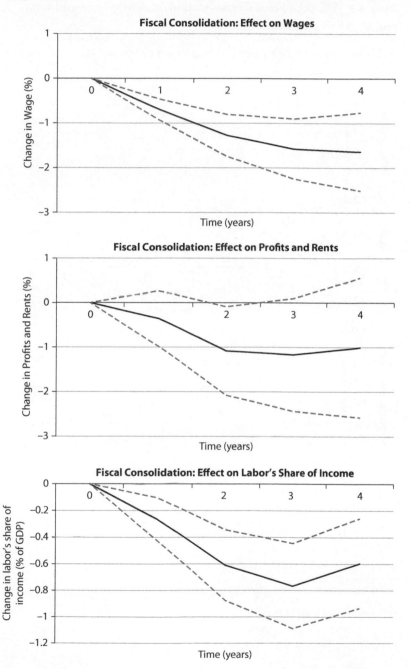

Source: Ball, Furceri, Leigh, and Loungani (2013).

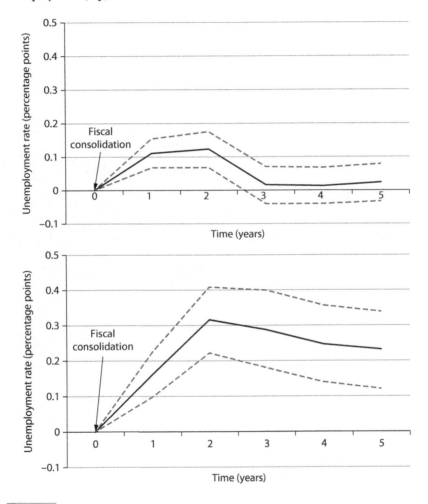

FIGURE 6.5: **Effect of Fiscal Consolidation on Short-Term and Long-Term Unemployment**

Fiscal consolidations raise long-term unemployment (bottom) more than short-term unemployment (top).

Note: The dotted lines are one-standard-error bands.

Source: Ball, Leigh, and Loungani (2011).

Fiscal consolidations thus add to the pain of those who are likely to be already suffering the most—the long-term unemployed. This is a particular worry today because the share of long-term unemployed increased in most OECD countries during the Great Recession. And even in countries where it did not increase—such as Germany, France, Italy, and Japan—the share had already been very high even before the recession. Job loss is associated with persistent earnings loss, adverse impacts on health, and declines in the academic performance and earnings potential of the children of displaced workers (Dao and Loungani 2010). These adverse impacts are exacerbated the longer a person is unemployed. Moreover, long spells of unemployment reduce the odds of being rehired. For instance, in the United States, a person unemployed for over six months had only a 1 in 10 chance of being rehired in the next month, compared with 1 in 3 odds for a person unemployed less than one month. The increase in long-term unemployment thus carries the risk of entrenching unemployment as a structural problem because workers lose skills and become detached from the labor force—a phenomenon referred to as *hysteresis*.

Long-term unemployment also threatens social cohesion. An opinion survey conducted in sixty-nine countries around the world found that an experience with unemployment leads to more negative opinions about the effectiveness of democracy and increases the desire for a rogue leader. The effects were found to be more pronounced for the long-term unemployed.

BALANCING COSTS AND BENEFITS

This chapter has examined the distributional effects of fiscal austerity. Episodes of fiscal consolidation for a sample of seventeen OECD countries over the past three decades have typically led to a significant and persistent increase in inequality, declines in wage income and in the wage share of income, and increases in long-term unemployment. These results are not confined to advanced economies; subsequent work by other authors has shown that inequality in emerging markets and low-income economies also increases in the aftermath of fiscal consolidation (Woo et al. 2017). The research described here shows that it is important to have realistic expectations about the short-term consequences of fiscal consolidation: it is likely to lower incomes—hitting wage-earners more than others—and raise unemployment, particularly long-term unemployment.

The notion that fiscal consolidations can be expansionary (i.e., raise output and employment), championed, among others, in the academic world by Harvard economist Alberto Alesina or in the policy world by former European Central Bank President Jean-Claude Trichet, has been seriously debunked. Instead, the short-run costs must be balanced against the potential longer-term benefits that consolidation can confer.

It is also important to be clear about the long-term benefits of paying down the debt when countries have fiscal space. There is little theoretical basis for setting a public debt target at some particular level (such as 60 percent of GDP under Maastricht or the 90 percent of GDP threshold discussed in Reinhart and Rogoff 2010). The seminal contributions from the economics literature point in all directions, from an ever-rising optimal level of public debt (if governments lack the ability to commit to future policies) to the accumulation of a large portfolio of assets (negative debt) to cope for adverse shocks under a precautionary saving motive. In its policy advice, the IMF has been more concerned with the *pace* of fiscal consolidation, ensuring that the pace is not too slow to give markets concern but not too fast to derail recovery. Hence, while the IMF has not questioned the need to bring down public debt ratios in the advanced countries from their high levels, it has not pushed for quick attainment of a particular public debt target.

CHAPTER 7

CENTRAL BANKS AND INEQUALITY

Income inequality in advanced economies has drawn the attention of prominent central bankers. Former U.S. Federal Reserve Chair Janet Yellen (2014) said that the "extent of and continuing increase in inequality in the United States greatly concern me." European Central Bank President Mario Draghi (2016) noted that "in advanced economies the real incomes of those in the lower half of the distribution have remained at the same level as a few decades ago." But do central bank actions themselves contribute to inequality?

The previous chapters have identified a long list of policies that have led to increases in income inequality—various structural policies, financial openness, and austerity. A decade ago, the policies of central banks would probably not have made this list: their actions were starting to be perceived as having impacts on the economy as a whole but discussions of their distributional effects—which had been prominent in the 1980s—were starting to fade.

Over the past decade, however, the distributional impacts of central bank actions have again become a topic of debate. Many central banks have kept policy interest rates at historical lows over this time to help bring income back to trend and inflation back to target. Some allege that this unprecedented easing of monetary policy has also raised income inequality. Acemoglu and Johnson (2012), for instance, argue that the financial sector benefits from lower interest rates because they have a positive impact on stock prices, thus boosting "the bonuses of top bankers and other chief executives."

As former U.S. Federal Reserve Chair Ben Bernanke (2015) notes, the distributional consequences of monetary policy are not easy to sort out because they operate through many channels. Nakajima (2015) provides a useful discussion of four important channels, two operating through the impacts on income and two through the impacts of unexpected inflation:

> *Wage heterogeneity channel:* the differential impact of monetary policy on incomes of different groups of workers across sectors of the economy—this was the debate in the United States in the 1980s, when there were debates that the Fed's actions were hurting low- and middle-income workers, particularly in the manufacturing sector;
> *Income composition channel:* the differential impact on wages versus financial income—this is the channel emphasized by Acemoglu and Johnson;
> *Effects on assets and debt:* Unexpected inflation can have differential impacts based on what kind of assets or debt people hold;
> *Portfolio composition channel:* Unexpected inflation also transfers wealth from households with nominal assets to those with nominal debt.

Because there are many channels, and they do not all operate in the same direction, figuring out the overall impact is an empirical issue. This is the view taken by Coibion et al. (2012), who study the impacts of the Fed's actions of the distribution of income in the United States. They find that, contrary to the fears often expressed, an easing of monetary policies by the Fed lowers income inequality across households.

MEASURING CENTRAL BANK ACTIONS

Our analysis here describes the impacts of central bank actions on income inequality in a broad group of countries, a total of thirty-two advanced economies and emerging market countries over the period of 1990–2013.

At the very outset, a distinction has to be made between the central bank's typical ("systematic" or "endogenous" in the jargon) responses to economic developments and those that are deviations from the typical response and hence are likely to come as a surprise. For instance, central banks typically lower interest rates as economies go into a slump; any changes in inequality that occur over this time could simply be the result of the slump in the economy rather than the central bank actions that it called forth. To isolate the impacts of monetary policy on inequality, one therefore has to strip away this typical response and capture the element of surprise in central bank actions. Economists call this the "exogenous" or "shock" component of monetary policy.

For the case of the United States, Romer and Romer (2004) devised a novel method to isolate the surprise component of the Fed's actions. They measured the extent to which changes in the Fed's policy interest rates could be accounted for by changes in the forecasts of output and inflation made by Fed staff; this could be taken as the systematic response of monetary policy. The residual was the surprise—the exogenous component of interest rate changes. It was this surprise component that was used by Coibion et al. (2012) to show that the Fed's easing led to declines in U.S. income inequality.

We faced the challenge of extending this method in a consistent fashion to a large group of countries. This required some adjustments, which are discussed in detail in Furceri, Loungani, and Zdzienicka (2017). But, in essence, we applied the Romer and Romer method, except that our forecasts of output and inflation came from a publication called *Consensus Forecasts* rather than from the forecasts made by the staff of the various central banks. This publication is a widely used source of forecasts, and the forecasts reported here are generally fairly close to those made by government agencies (in cases where government forecasts are easily available).

Figure 7.1 compares the exogenous component of U.S. monetary policy using our method with that used by Romer and Romer. Reassuringly, the two are very close, raising the odds that our method works well for the other countries as well.

THE EFFECTS OF MONETARY POLICY

We then look at the impacts of these surprise elements of central bank actions on the overall economy and on the distribution of income—the Gini coefficient, the labor share of income, and the share of income going to the top percentiles.

The effects on the overall economy are shown in figure 7.2. An easing of monetary policy (lowering of policy interest rates) raises output and inflation,

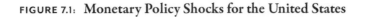

FIGURE 7.1: Monetary Policy Shocks for the United States

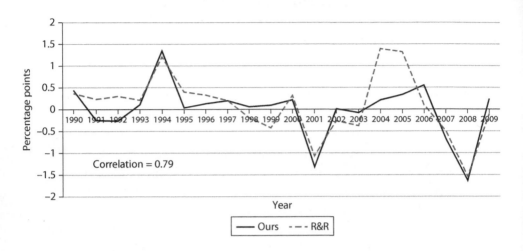

Note: "Ours" refers to the monetary policy shocks identified using the procedure described in the text. "R&R" refers to the monetary policy shocks identified by Romer and Romer (2004).

consistent with what other studies have found using data for individual countries. It is reassuring that our measures of monetary policy actions have effects on the overall economy that are similar to what other methods deliver. The easing of monetary policy also raises house prices and equity prices, as Acemoglu and Johnson (2012) conjectured was the case.

However, the increase in house and equity prices does not lead to increases in overall income inequality. Instead, it turns out that the findings of Coibion et al. for the United States hold for other countries as well: a 100 basis-point surprise decline in the policy rate lowers the Gini measure of inequality by about 1.25 percent in the short term and by about 2.25 percent in the medium term. This is shown in figure 7.3. The effect is economically significant: the magnitude of the medium-term effect is approximately equivalent to one standard deviation of the change in the Gini coefficient (2.4 percent) in the sample.

Other measures of inequality support this finding—the labor share of income rises (figure 7.4) and the shares of income going to the top 10 percent, 5 percent, and 1 percent all fall (figure 7.5).

FIGURE 7.2: The Effects of Unanticipated Monetary Policy Easing

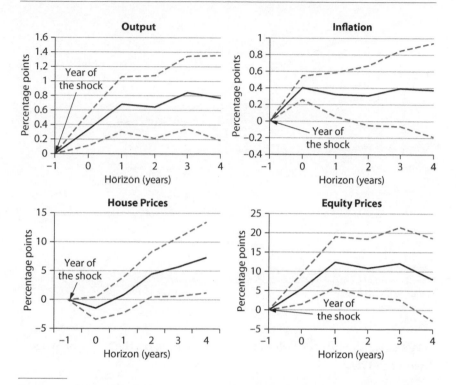

Note: t = 0 is the year of the shock. Solid lines denote the response to an unanticipated monetary policy rate decline of 100 basis points, and dashed lines denote 90 percent confidence bands.

To summarize, our results provide very clear-cut evidence that exogenous monetary policy easing lowers inequality. Previous studies for particular countries have not found such clear evidence, or have expected results to go in the other direction. We suspect this is the case for a couple of reasons. First, some authors have used changes in policy interest rates and have not distinguished between the systematic and exogenous components of policy. This tends to give small effects of monetary policy on the Gini coefficient, as shown in figure 7.6 (top panel). Second, if the systematic component of monetary policy is used, central bank easing is associated with an increase in inequality, the direction that some authors have expected (figure 7.6, bottom panel). However, because

The Effects of Unanticipated Monetary Policy Easing on Income Inequality

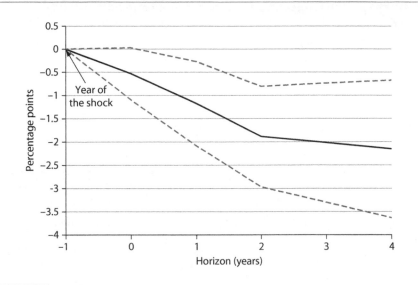

Note: t = 0 is the year of the shock. Solid lines denote the response to an unanticipated monetary policy rate decline of 100 basis points, and dashed lines denote 90 percent confidence bands.

FIGURE 7.4: **The Effect of Monetary Policy Easing on the Share of Wage Income in GDP**

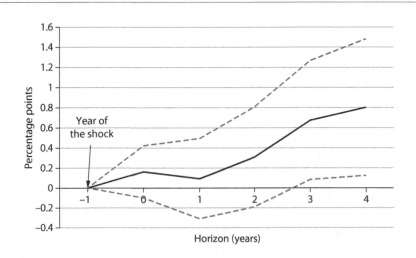

Note: t = 0 is the year of the shock. Solid lines denote the response to an unanticipated monetary policy rate decline of 100 basis points, and dashed lines denote 90 percent confidence bands.

FIGURE 7.5: The Effect of Monetary Policy Easing on Top Income Shares

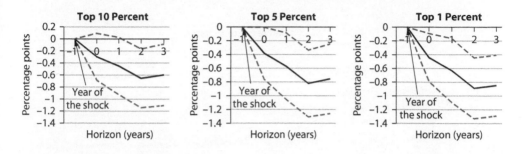

Note: t = 0 is the year of the shock. Solid lines denote the response to an unanticipated monetary policy rate decline of 100 basis points, and dashed lines denote 90 percent confidence bands.

these systematic interest rate changes come about in response to a slumping economy, it is likely that the increase in inequality arises because of the effects of deteriorating economic conditions rather than the central bank actions.

IMPLICATIONS FOR CENTRAL BANKS

As Voinea and Monnin (2017) note, central bankers had started to forget about any possible links of monetary policy on inequality. However, the very accommodative monetary policies followed since the onset of the Great Recession, combined with concerns over rising inequality, have brought about open discussions of distributional impacts. Our results point to the importance of making a distinction between the systematic component of policy and monetary policy shocks. We find that expansionary monetary policy shocks lower income inequality.

As central banks contemplate a liftoff from very low interest rates, they may want to be aware of the distributional impacts of their actions for a couple of reasons. First, as Voinea and Monnin (2017) write, "solving inequality is certainly not the primary job of central banks, but it is a factor that they should not ignore. Securing balanced growth and a fair distribution of the benefits and costs of price stability . . . is a public good, too."

FIGURE 7.6: The Effect of Monetary Policy Easing: Exogenous vs. Growth-Driven Shocks and Change in Policy Rates

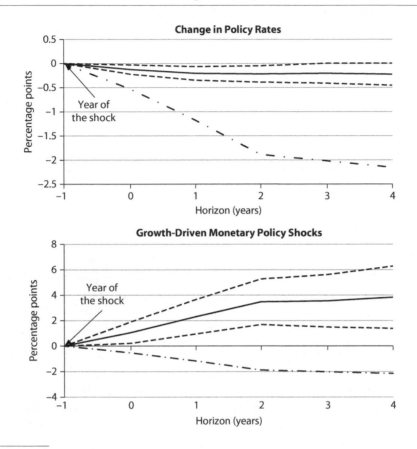

Note: t = 0 is the year of the shock. Solid lines denote the response to, alternatively, a growth-driven increase or changes in monetary policy rates of 100 basis points; dashed lines denote 90 percent confidence bands. Dash-dot lines denote the unconditional (baseline) response presented in figure 7.3. Growth-driven monetary policy shocks are identified as the forecast error in policy rates explained by news in growth and inflation. Innovations in policy rates are the forecast error in policy rates.

Second, recent research suggests that the distribution of income—and changes in that distribution—may itself affect how monetary policy affects the economy. Hence, even if the central bank is primarily concerned with the aggregate effects of its policies, understanding the impacts of policies on inequality may be important.

CHAPTER 8

TECHNOLOGY, ROBOTS, AND INEQUALITY

The world may be entering a "second machine age." Every week we read about a new application of artificial intelligence, so-called deep learning, and robotic technology. Automated delivery trucks, electronic teaching and scheduling assistants, computers that replace paralegals, and self-driving cars are just a few examples. Some seem to resemble the "robot" envisioned by Czech science fiction writer Karel Čapek, who coined the term in 1921 to describe an intelligent machine essentially indistinguishable from a human.

We saw in chapter 2 that technology has been an important contributor to inequality (figure 2.8). But technological advances are also the source of long-run growth. Balancing the efficiency and equity effects of technology has been a perennial challenge for societies, one that is likely to get worse with the spread of robots.

Two narratives have emerged in the economic literature on technology, growth, and distribution. One says that, despite some transition costs as particular jobs become obsolete, the overall effect of technological change is a much higher standard of living. The history of this debate since at least the nineteenth century seems to yield a decisive victory for technological optimists. The average American worker in 2015 worked roughly 17 weeks to live at the annual income level of the average worker in 1915—and technology was a huge part of that progress (Autor 2015).

This optimistic narrative points to the many ways that technology does much more than displace workers. It makes workers more productive and raises demand for their services—for example, mapping software makes taxi (and now Lyft and Uber) drivers more efficient. And rising incomes generate demand for all sorts of outputs and hence labor. A wave of fear about the implications of computerization for jobs surged in the United States in the 1950s and early 1960s, but subsequent decades of strong productivity growth and rising standards of living saw roughly stable unemployment and rising employment.

The other, more pessimistic, narrative pays more attention to the losers (see, for example, Sachs and Kotlikoff 2012; Ford 2015; Freeman 2015). Some of the increased inequality in many advanced economies in recent decades may result from technological pressure. The computer revolution has reduced relative demand in developed economies for jobs involving routinized work (physical or mental)—think bookkeeper or factory line worker. Because computers combined with a smaller number of—generally more skilled—workers have been able to produce the goods previously associated with these jobs, relative wages for people with fewer skills have fallen in many countries.

ROBOTS AND THE CAPITAL SHARE OF INCOME

Should the spread of intelligent robots lead us toward the optimistic narrative or the pessimistic one? Unlike our approach in previous chapters, which was empirical (i.e., drew on data from the past), we designed an economic model to help us think through the answer to this question, recognizing that past may not be prologue in this case (see Berg, Buffie, and Zanna 2018 for a model along these lines).

Macroeconomists usually think of production as resulting from the combination of physical capital stock (comprising machines and structures, both public and private) and labor. Our model assumes robots to be a different sort of capital, one that is a close substitute for human workers. Production will still require buildings and roads, for example, but now people and robots can work with this traditional capital.

So what happens when this robot capital gets productive enough to be useful? If we assume that robots are almost perfect substitutes for human labor, the good news is that output per person rises. The bad news is that inequality worsens, for several reasons. First, robots increase the supply of total effective (workers plus robots) labor, which drives down wages in a market-driven economy. Second, because it is now profitable to invest in robots, there is a shift away from investment in traditional capital, such as buildings and conventional machinery. This further lowers the demand for those who work with that traditional capital.

But this is just the beginning. Both the good and bad news intensify over time. As the stock of robots increases, so does the return on traditional capital (warehouses are more useful with robot shelf stockers). Eventually, therefore, traditional investment picks up too. This in turn keeps robots productive, even as the stock of robots continues to grow. Over time, the two types of capital grow together until they increasingly dominate the entire economy. All this traditional and robot capital, with diminishing help from labor, produces more and more output. And robots are not expected to consume, just produce (though the science fiction literature is ambiguous about this!). So there is more and more output to be shared among actual people.

However, wages fall, not just in relative terms but also absolutely, even as output grows. This may sound odd, or even paradoxical. How can we explain the fall in wages coinciding with the growing output? To put it another way, who buys all the higher output? The owners of capital do. In the short run, higher investment more than counterbalances any temporary decline in consumption. In the long run, the share of capital owners in the growing pie—and their consumption spending—is itself growing. With falling wages and rising capital stocks, (human) labor becomes a smaller and smaller part of the economy. Piketty, Saez, and Zucman (2016) have reminded us that the capital share is a basic determinant of income distribution. Capital is already much more unevenly distributed than income in all countries. The introduction of robots would further drive up the capital share, so the income distribution would tend to grow ever more uneven.

So far, we've assumed nearly perfect substitutability between robots and workers along with a small increase in robot efficiency. These are robots of the sort featured in the Hollywood movie *Terminator 2: Judgment Day*—such perfect substitutes for humans that they are indistinguishable. Another plausible scenario departs from both these assumptions. It is more realistic, at least for now, to assume that robots and human labor are close but not perfect substitutes, that people bring a spark of creativity or a critical human touch. At the same time, like some technologists, we project that robot productivity increases not just a little but dramatically over a span of a couple of decades.

With these assumptions, we recover a bit of the economist's typical optimism, as shown in figure 8.1. The forces mentioned before are still at play: robot capital tends to replace workers and drive down wages, and at first the diversion of investment into robots dries up the supplies of traditional capital that help raise wages. The difference, though, is that humans' special talents become increasingly valuable and productive as they combine with this gradually accumulating traditional and robot capital. Eventually, this increase in labor productivity outweighs the fact that the robots are replacing humans, and wages (as well as output) rise.

But there are two problems. First, "eventually" can be a long time coming. Exactly how long depends on how easy it is to substitute robots for human labor, and how quickly savings and investment respond to rates of return. According to our model's baseline scenario shown in figure 8.1, it

FIGURE 8.1: Effect of Increased Robot Efficiency on Wages, Income, and Income Shares

An increase in the efficiency of robots eventually raises wages—after twenty years—but lowers labor's share of income.

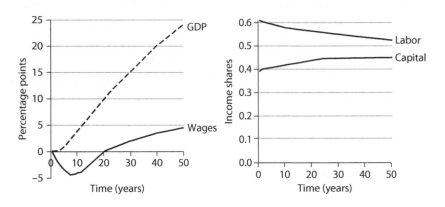

Note: For wages (dashed line) and GDP (solid line), the left panel shows deviation from initial steady state in percentage points. The x-axis shows time in years. The elasticity of substitution between "robot" capital and labor is assumed to be 2.5. See Berg, Buffie, and Zanna (2018) for details and various alternative scenarios. The specific assumption is that the elasticity of substitution between workers and "robot" capital is 2.5, meaning that a 1 percent increase in the wage would increase the ratio of robot capital to labor by 2.5 percent, holding constant other prices and the quantity of traditional capital. Details and many alternative scenarios are presented in Berg, Buffie, and Zanna (2018).

takes twenty years for the productivity effect to outweigh the substitution effect and drive up wages. Second, capital will still likely greatly increase its role in the economy. It will not completely take over as it does in the singularity case, but it will take a higher share of income, even in the long run when wages are above the pre-robot-era level. Thus, inequality will be worse, possibly dramatically so.

ROBOTS AND LABOR INCOME INEQUALITY

In addition to changing the relative shares of labor and capital income, robots may exacerbate income inequality among workers. This is because not all labor is the same. We recognize this by extending our model to divide all workers into two categories, which we call "skilled" and "unskilled." By skilled we mean that they are not close substitutes for robots; rather, robots may increase their productivity. By unskilled we mean that they are very close substitutes. Thus, our skilled workers may not be the traditionally highly educated; they may be those with creativity or empathy, which is particularly hard for future robots to match. We assume, following Frey and Osborne (2013), that about half of the labor force can be replaced by robots and is thus "unskilled."

What happens now when robot technology becomes cheaper? As before, output per person grows (figure 8.2). And the share of overall capital (robots plus traditional) rises. Now, though, there is an additional effect: the wages of skilled workers rise relative to those of the unskilled—and absolutely. Why? Because these workers are more productive when combined with robots. Imagine, for example, the greater productivity of a designer who now commands an army of robots. Meanwhile, the wages of the unskilled collapse, both in relative and in absolute terms, even over the long run.

Inequality now increases for two fundamental reasons. As before, capital receives a greater share of total income. In addition, wage inequality worsens dramatically. Productivity and real wages paid to skilled labor increase steadily, but low-skilled workers wage a lonely battle against the robots and lose badly. The numbers depend on a few key parameters, such as the degree of complementarity between skilled workers and robots, but the rough magnitude of the outcome follows from the simple assumptions we have laid out. We find that over a period of fifty miserable years, the real wage for low-skilled labor

FIGURE 8.2: Effect of Increased Robot Efficiency on Wages of Skilled and Unskilled Workers

Increased robot efficiency lowers wages of unskilled workers and their share of income

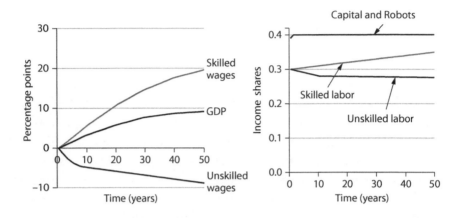

Note: This figure follows the same assumptions as figure 8.1, except that now "robot" capital is assumed to complement workers with a college degree ("skilled workers") and substitute for unskilled workers. See Berg, Buffie, and Zanna (2018) for details and various alternative scenarios.

decreases 40 percent, and the group's share in national income drops from 35 percent to about 10 percent in our baseline scenario.

So far, we have been thinking of a large developed economy, such as the United States. And this seems natural given that such countries tend to be more advanced technologically. However, a robot age could also affect the international distribution of output. For example, if the unskilled labor replaced by robots resembles the workforce of developing economies, it could lower those countries' relative wages.

WHO WILL OWN THE ROBOTS?

These stories are not destiny. First, we are mainly speculating about the outcome of emerging technological trends, not analyzing existing data. Recent innovations we have in mind have not (yet) shown up in productivity or growth statistics in developed economies; productivity growth has in fact been low in recent years. And, as we have noted, technology is not the only—or even the main—culprit for the rise in inequality in many countries. In most advanced economies growth in the relative wages of skilled workers has been smaller than in the United States, even in advanced economies presumably facing similar technological changes. As Piketty, Saez, and Zucman (2016) have famously emphasized, much of the increase in inequality in recent decades is concentrated in a very small fraction of the population, and technology does not seem to be the main story. But the rising inequality observed in so many parts of the world over recent decades—and perhaps even some of the political instability and populism in the news—underscores the risks and raises the stakes. And it is ominous that the labor share of income in the United States seems to have been falling since the turn of the century, after decades of rough stability (Freeman 2015).

Science fiction writer Isaac Asimov's famous three laws of robotics were designed to protect people from physical harm by robots. According to the first law, "A robot may not injure a human being or, through inaction, allow a human being to come to harm." Such guidance may be fine for designers of individual robots, but it would do little to manage the economy-wide consequences we discuss here. Our little model shows that, even in a smoothly functioning market economy, robots may be profitable for owners of capital and may raise average per capita income, but the result would not be the kind of society in which most of us would want to live. The case for a public policy response is strong.

In all these scenarios, there are jobs for people who want to work. The problem is that most of the income goes to owners of capital and to skilled workers who cannot easily be replaced by robots. Other people get low wages and a shrinking share of the pie. This points to the importance of education that promotes the sort of creativity and skills that will complement—not be replaced by—intelligent machines. Such investment in human capital could raise average wages and lower inequality. But even so, the introduction of robots may depress average wages for a long time, and the capital share will rise.

Such a society would face many challenges. These could include ensuring sufficient aggregate demand when buying power is increasingly concentrated, addressing the social and political challenges associated with such low wages and high inequality, and dealing with the implications of lower wages when it comes to workers' ability to pay for health care and education and invest in their children. Is there a way out? Yes. We have implicitly assumed so far that income from capital remains highly unequally distributed. But the increase in overall output per person implies that everyone could be better off if income from capital is redistributed. One way is to guarantee a basic income for all, financed by capital taxation. But there are other mechanisms for redistribution. What is undeniable is that redistribution has to be a big part of the policy agenda not just to tackle the inequality that exists at present but the even sharper inequality that may be coming with the spread of robots.

CHAPTER 9

REMEDIES FOR INEQUALITY—
REDISTRIBUTION

We have seen that equality drives higher and more sustainable growth. That does not in itself support efforts to redistribute. In particular, inequality may impede growth at least in part *because* it calls forth efforts to redistribute that themselves undercut growth. In such a situation, even if inequality is bad for growth, taxes and transfers may be precisely the wrong remedy. The negative effect of redistributive policies—the efficiency "leaks" that efforts to reduce inequality engender—is indeed a central theme of Arthur Okun's famous 1975 book *Equality and Efficiency: The Big Trade-off.*

But there are arguments on the other side too. Equality-enhancing interventions could actually help growth. Examples could include taxes on activities with negative externalities paid mostly by the better-off but harmful to the poor (such as, perhaps, excessive risk-taking in the financial sector), cash transfers aimed at encouraging better attendance at primary schools in developing countries, or spending on public capital or education that benefits the poor. Some categories of government spending—for example, public investments in infrastructure, spending on health and education, and social insurance provision—may be both pro-growth and pro-equality, whereas other categories may imply the trade-offs that preoccupied Okun. The macroeconomic effects of redistributive policies are likely to reflect a balance between different components of the fiscal package, and it would appear to be an empirical question whether redistribution in practice is pro-growth or anti-growth. Hence we should not jump to the conclusion that the treatment for inequality is worse for growth than the disease itself: there could be win-win policies that have potential to promote both efficiency *and* equality.

A large literature has examined the interrelationship between redistribution, growth, and inequality, resulting in a complex set of proposed relationships summarized in figure 9.1. Inequality can influence growth (line E) positively by providing incentives for innovation and entrepreneurship (Lazear and Rosen 1981); by raising saving and investment if rich people save a higher fraction of their income; and, perhaps especially relevant for poor countries, by allowing at least a few individuals to accumulate the minimum needed to start businesses and get a good education (Barro 2000). But inequality may be harmful for growth because it deprives the poor of the ability to stay healthy and accumulate human capital (Perotti 1996; Galor and Moav 2004; Aghion, Caroli, and García-Peñalosa 1999); generates political and economic instability that reduces investment (Alesina and Perotti 1996); and impedes the social consensus required to adjust to shocks and sustain growth (Rodrik 1999, a). The relationship between inequality and growth may be nonlinear, as in the theoretical model of Benhabib (2003), in which increases in inequality from low levels provide growth-enhancing incentives, while increases past some point encourage rent-seeking and lower growth.

On the relationship between market inequality and redistribution (line A), we emphasize the channel underscored in the seminal paper of Meltzer and Richard (1981), who argue that higher inequality will create pressures for redistribution. The notion is that, at least in democracies, political power is more evenly distributed than economic power, so a majority of voters will have the power and incentive to vote for redistribution. However, as emphasized by Stiglitz (2015), this need not be the case if the rich have more political influence than the poor.

On whether redistribution affects growth (line D), it has been generally assumed that it hurts growth (Okun 1975), as higher taxes and subsidies dampen incentives to work and invest. But some have recognized that redistribution need not be inherently detrimental to growth, to the degree that it involves reducing tax expenditures or loopholes that benefit the rich or as part of broader tax reforms (such as higher inheritance taxes offset by lower taxes on labor income). More broadly, redistribution can also occur when progressive taxes finance public investment, when social insurance spending enhances the welfare of the poor and risk-taking (Benabou 2000), or when

FIGURE 9.1: Interrelationships Between Inequality, Redistribution, and Growth

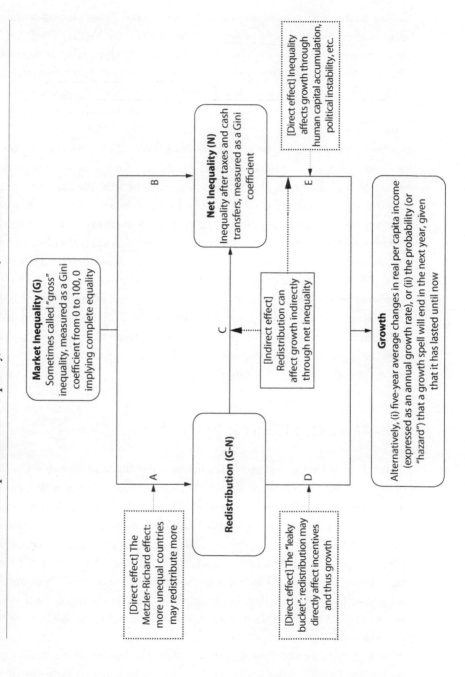

higher health and education spending benefits the poor, helping to offset labor and capital market imperfections (Saint-Paul and Verdier 1993, 1997). In such cases, redistributive policies could increase both equality and growth. The literature has generally ignored the overall effects of redistribution, that is by combining direct effects (line D) and indirect effects through inequality (lines C and E), because very few papers look simultaneously at both inequality and redistribution.

The empirical studies on the relation between redistribution and growth are also somewhat divided. Tanzi and Zee (1997) find some general indication that the relationship between growth and the level of taxes is negative but that this relationship is not robust and is sensitive to model specification. With respect to spending, Lindert (2004) sees something of a "free lunch" paradox in that some categories of public spending that are redistributive have no apparent adverse impact on growth (for example, spending on health and education, or tax-financed infrastructure spending).

Our approach here is to tackle the question head-on: what does the historical macroeconomic evidence say about the relationship between inequality, redistribution, and growth? In particular, can we find evidence that, on average, the negative growth effects of inequality outweigh any positive growth effects of the resulting reduction in inequality?

MEASURING REDISTRIBUTION

A defining constraint of previous studies on inequality and growth is the lack of data on both net and market inequality measures on a comparable basis for a large number of countries. This has made it difficult for researchers to distinguish between the effects of inequality and those of redistribution. There are numerous problems with the quality and coverage of the surveys, particularly for developing countries and in the more distant past. But perhaps the most salient issue is that while there are many household surveys of distribution, they are generally not comparable. For example, some measure income per capita and some per household; some try to measure disposable income, and others measure total spending.

Solt (2016) represents the best effort so far to address these problems, combining information from available surveys to infer comparable series of the

Gini coefficient for net and market inequality for as many countries and as many years as possible. He assembles inequality measures from available surveys, making a judgment about when the quality of the survey is good enough to warrant inclusion in the dataset.

Using Solt's data, we define redistribution as the difference between market and net inequality. Table 9.1 presents correlations between our measure of redistribution and a number of proxies that have been used in the earlier literature. The table shows that the correlations are in the range of about one-half to three-quarters. We find it reassuring both that our measure is highly correlated with many common-sense direct measures of transfers, and that it may also contain unique information (because the correlation is well below 100 percent). This is consistent with the observation that many presumptively redistributive transfers may not be so in particular cases. It also may reflect the fact that net inequality in Solt (2009) does not generally capture the effects of in-kind provision of goods and services by the government or of indirect taxes, because these are not usually captured in the underlying household surveys.

We now take a first look at the trends on inequality and redistribution. Do countries with higher market inequality tend to redistribute more? Figure 9.2

TABLE 9.1: Correlation Between Redistribution and Transfers

Name of Transfers Variable	Correlation Coefficient
Tax revenue (% of GDP) (WBWDI)	0.51
Subsidies and other transfers (% of expense) (WBWDI)	0.49
Social security benefits paid by general government/ GDP (OECD)	0.55
Current transfers received by households/GDP (OECD)	0.52
Subsidies/GDP (OECD)	0.42
Social expenditure in percentage of GDP (OECD)	0.68
Total tax revenue as percentage of GDP (OECD)	0.70

Note: Redistribution is calculated as the difference between market and net income inequality.

Source: Ostry, Berg, and Tsangarides (2014).

Most countries lie below the 45-degree line, implying some degree of redistribution.

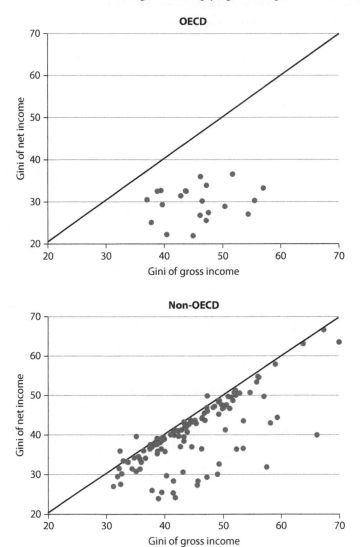

Note: The Gini coefficient for net income inequality is on the y-axis, and the Gini for market income inequality is on the x-axis (both for the latest year data were available). The distance below the solid diagonal line represents the amount of redistribution.

Source: Ostry, Berg, and Tsangarides (2014).

Note: Latest available year of market and net inequality; the line represents the 45-degree line.

Source: Ostry, Berg, and Tsangarides (2014).

compares net inequality on the y-axis with market inequality on the x-axis (each point represents one country in the latest year for which data are available). A country on the 45-degree line would have identical net and market inequality. Most countries lie below the line, implying some degree of redistribution, and a few carry out a substantial amount of redistribution. OECD countries engage in a larger amount of redistribution than do non-OECD countries. Indeed, in this group, countries with relatively high market inequality have only slightly above-average net inequality (the points in the panel are clustered roughly along a horizontal line). One way to put it is that relatively unequal countries are those that have a small amount of redistribution given their level of market inequality.

Our results confirm a significant relationship between market inequality and redistribution. The estimated effect is substantial: an increase in market inequality from the fiftieth to the seventy-fifth percentile of the sample (that is, from a market Gini of 45 such as the Philippines in 2005 to 51 such as Nicaragua in 2005) is associated with an increase in redistribution by 3 percentage points. The relationship is much stronger in the OECD sample than in the rest of the sample, where it is nonetheless still significant.   M - R proven

REDISTRIBUTION AND GROWTH

We now take a look at the evidence on the relationship between growth on the one hand and inequality and redistribution on the other, using two approaches. First, we follow the literature and examine medium-term growth and our variables of interest. Specifically, we ask how average growth over a five-year period depends on a variety of indicators, including the level of income, the quality of institutions, and especially important in our setting, the level of inequality and extent of redistributive transfers. Second, we look at the duration of growth spells that were the focus at chapter 3. We can observe in figure 9.3 that there] simple is at best a weak (and slightly negative) relationship between redistribution ┘ and the duration of growth.

As in previous chapters, it is important to go beyond simple correlations. Much else is at play in driving growth. Moreover, we know that our variables of interest are themselves interrelated. Thus, we need to see how the relationships hold up when both inequality and redistribution are included simultaneously, and with the inclusion of other factors.

FIGURE 9.3: **Growth and Redistribution**

There is at best a weak (and slightly negative) relationship between redistribution and growth.

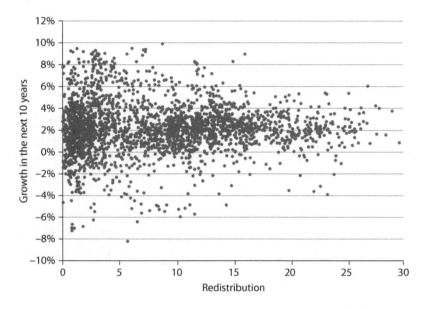

Note: Simple correlations between growth in the next ten years, and the average net income inequality and transfers for a sample of countries.

Source: Ostry, Berg, and Tsangarides (2014).

direct

Our basic specification is a simple model in which growth depends on initial income, net inequality, and redistribution. The results from our analysis are shown graphically in figure 9.4. The height of the bar represents the effect on the growth rate of increasing the value of the variable in question from the median value in the sample to the sixtieth percentile. We find that *indirect* higher inequality lowers growth. Quantitatively, an increase in net Gini from 37 (such as in the United States in 2005) to 42 (such as in Gabon in 2005) decreases growth on average by 0.5 percentage points, that is, from 5 percent to 4.5 percent per year, holding redistribution and initial income constant. Redistribution, in contrast, has virtually no effect on output. Adding these two effects gives us the total effect of an increase in redistribution on growth.

FIGURE 9.4: The Effect of Inequality and Redistribution on Growth

Higher inequality lowers growth.

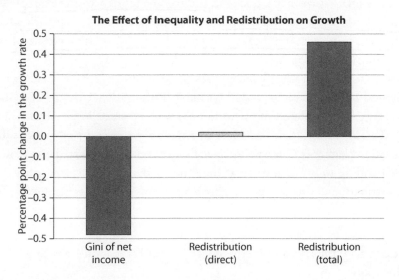

Note: For each variable, the height of the bar shows the increase in the five-year average real per capita income growth associated with an increase in that variable from the fiftieth to the sixtieth percentile, with other variables at the fiftieth percentile. The lighter shade of the redistribution bar reflects the fact that this effect is imprecisely estimated and is not significantly different from zero. The calculation of the total effect of redistribution assumes that redistribution has no effect on market inequality.

Source: Ostry, Berg, and Tsangarides (2014).

This total effect is the sum of (1) the direct effect from changing redistribution while keeping the net Gini constant, plus (2) the growth impact of the resulting decline in net Gini. The net effect is to increase the annual growth rate by about 0.5 percentage points.

These results are inconsistent with the notion that there is on average a major trade-off between a reduction of inequality through redistribution and growth. If there *were* such a trade-off, redistribution should have a negative impact on growth and in fact an impact that is stronger than that of net inequality. If that were the case, then redistribution that reduced inequality would on average be bad for growth, taking into account both the direct effect of higher redistribution and the effect of the resulting lower inequality.

Our results decisively reject that hypothesis: <u>net inequality clearly has an adverse impact on growth while redistribution has virtually no impact.</u> This implies that, rather than a trade-off, <u>the average result across the sample is a win-win situation, in which redistribution has an overall progrowth effect, counting both potential negative direct effects and positive effects of the resulting lower inequality.</u>

Our results hold when standard growth determinants are included, such as physical and human capital as well as a number of additional determinants such as external shocks, the quality of institutions, and measures of openness to trade.

We now turn to growth spells and estimate the hazard probabilities discussed in chapter 3. Our baseline specification relates the hazard of a growth spell ending to initial income at the start of the spell, and inequality and redistribution during the spell. Figure 9.5 presents our results graphically. We

FIGURE 9.5: The Effect of Increasing Different Factors on Growth Spell Duration

Inequality has a statistically significant negative relationship with the duration of growth spells.

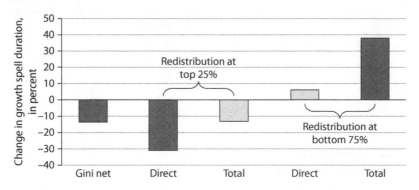

Note: For redistribution, the height of the first column shows the percentage increase in spell duration resulting from an increase in redistribution from the seventy-fifth to the eighty-fifth percentile, with all other variables at their median values. For the other variables, the height of the associated column shows the percentage increase in spell duration resulting from an increase in that variable from the fiftieth to the sixtieth percentile, with other variables at their median values. The lighter shade of the third and fourth bars reflects the fact that these effects are imprecisely estimated and are not significantly different from zero.

Source: Ostry, Berg, and Tsangarides (2014).

find that inequality has a statistically significant negative relationship with the duration of growth spells. This echoes the results of chapter 3, but now controlling for redistribution. Turning to redistribution, we find (shown as in the second and third bars of figure 9.5) that when redistribution is already high (at the top 25th percentile), there is evidence that further redistribution is indeed harmful to growth, as the Okun (1975) "big trade-off" hypothesis would suggest. When it is below that level, however, there is no evidence that further redistribution has any effect on growth.

Thus, as with the growth regressions, we find that, contrary to the big trade-off hypothesis, the overall effect of redistribution is pro-growth, with the possible exception of extremely large redistributions. There is no negative direct effect, and the resulting lower inequality seems to be associated with longer growth spells. For very large redistributions, the point estimate of the effect of redistribution on growth is negative and somewhat larger in absolute value than the estimated (positive) effect of inequality on growth, but this difference is statistically insignificant. This means that even in the case of large redistributions, there is little evidence of an overall adverse effect on growth, because the pro-equality and disincentive effects of the transfers roughly balance each other out. For smaller transfers, those of less than thirteen percentage points, the evidence suggests that the overall effect of redistribution would be growth-positive: roughly neutral direct effects of redistribution, and a protective effect of the resulting reduction in inequality. Here too, controlling for a number of potential determinants of growth spells preserves the results related to inequality. The results with respect to redistribution are more fragile. In particular, the negative effect of very large transfers seems to disappear when certain other factors are controlled for.

We see an important policy implication from our findings. Extreme caution about redistribution—and thus inaction—is unlikely to be appropriate in many cases. On average, across countries and over time, the things that governments have typically done to redistribute do not seem to have led to bad growth outcomes, unless they were extreme. And the resulting narrowing of inequality helped support faster and more durable growth.

CHAPTER 10

CONCLUSIONS

The field of macroeconomics was born in the aftermath of the Great Depression of the 1930s, when average incomes fell by 25 percent in some countries. Avoiding such a decline by using monetary and fiscal policies became the main concern of macroeconomists. In the 1980s, understanding why average incomes differed across countries became a second important topic of investigation. Over the past three decades, a consensus has emerged that a triad of policies—consisting of (1) macroeconomic discipline, (2) structural reforms to free up markets, and (3) the global spread of markets through free trade and movement of capital and labor—can deliver growth in average incomes and help the poorer countries catch up with the richer ones.

There is much to cheer about the substantial benefits generated by these policies. Global growth has increased in the 1990s and before the onset of the Great Recession was fairly robust, in particular in many populous countries such as China and India. As a result, between-country inequality has declined and millions have been rescued from abject poverty. The Millennium Development Goal of reduction in absolute poverty was met five years ahead of schedule. Inflation has been tamed in advanced economies and in many developing economies as well.

These substantial benefits, however, have not been equally shared. Median incomes have stagnated in the United States and in many other advanced economies, the labor share of income has steadily declined in many countries, and

within-country inequality has increased in almost all advanced econo.
in several emerging markets. The evidence in this book suggests that greater
attention to these distributional consequences of many economic policies is
needed. The reasons are three-fold.

First, excessive levels of inequality are bad not only for social and moral
reasons but also for growth and efficiency: although the relation between
inequality and growth can be complex, higher levels of inequality are associated, on average, with lower and less durable growth (Ostry 2015; Berg
and Ostry 2017). Hence, even from the perspective of the goal of fostering growth, attention to inequality is necessary. Moreover, high levels of
inequality may lead to latent social conflicts that ultimately translate into
political backlash against the pursuit of free market policies, including
globalization.

Second, the fear that redistribution will have an adverse impact on growth
turns out to find little support in the data—implementing policies to reduce
excessive inequality tends on average to support growth rather than to retard
it: "sharing wealth more equally may actually produce more wealth overall"
(Ostry 2014).

Third, many adverse distributional developments arise from policy choices
made by governments. Hence, they are not—as sometimes argued—exclusively
due to technological developments and other global trends beyond the control
of any one government.

For these reasons, we suggest a course correction in the rules of the road
that have governed economic policy making across much of the world. While
the pursuit of market-friendly policies is needed and desirable to ensure an
increase in average living standards, the distributional consequences of these
policies should be recognized and addressed ex-ante through better policy design—with aggregate *and* distributional effects in mind—and ex-post
through redistribution (Ostry, Furceri and Loungani, 2018).

A NEW GOAL: GOING FOR INCLUSIVE GROWTH

Happily, there is evidence that governments are paying greater attention to the
efficiency–equity trade-offs posed by economic policies. So rather than just

"going for growth"—as the consensus view and organizations like the OECD advocated as a goal—governments are opting for inclusive growth (Loungani 2017). Inclusion is important, but so of course is growth: "a larger slice of the pie for everyone calls for a bigger pie" (Lipton 2016). Hence, the advocates of inclusive growth do not have in mind as role models either the former Soviet Union or present-day North Korea—those are examples of inclusive misery, not inclusive growth.

The change in goal is reflected in the policy choices countries make and in the advice they get from institutions such as the IMF. For instance, on fiscal policy, the IMF's then-chief economist Olivier Blanchard said "what is needed in many advanced economies is a credible medium-term fiscal consolidation, not a fiscal noose today" (IMF Survey 2010). In October 2013, the IMF's managing director Christine Lagarde applauded the decision by the U.S. Congress to raise the country's debt ceiling. On the pace of U.S. fiscal consolidation, Lagarde advised: "we say slow down because the point is not to contract the economy by slashing spending brutally now as recovery is picking up" (Howell 2013). For the euro area, the IMF advocated that "those with fiscal space should use it to support investment" (IMF 2015).

Attitudes toward unfettered flows of foreign capital are also changing. The mounting evidence that some flows generate large costs but little benefit led the IMF's former first deputy managing director Stanley Fischer to exclaim: "What useful purpose is served by short-term international capital flows?" Among policymakers today, there is increased acceptance of using a variety of tools to mitigate the risks to financial stability and to the economy associated with capital flows, especially short-term carry trade flows (Ostry 2012). Greater exchange rate flexibility offers some insulation against the risks of volatile capital flows (Obstfeld, Ostry, and Qureshi 2018). But so do capital controls and prudential measures to restrain the financial sector (Ostry, Ghosh, Chamon, and Qureshi 2011, 2012). Capital controls may be the best option when it is borrowing from abroad that is the source of an unsustainable credit boom (Ostry, Ghosh, and Qureshi 2015).

The IMF also recognizes that opening up to foreign capital flows is generally more beneficial and less risky if countries have reached certain thresholds of financial and institutional development, and that full liberalization may not be the appropriate end goal for many countries (Ghosh, Ostry, and Qureshi 2017).

TOWARD AN INCLUSIVE GLOBALIZATION

Events over the past few years have prompted concerns about a reversal of globalization. That would only serve to negate the great benefits that freer trade has engendered, as we noted earlier. At the same time, not acknowledging some of the shortcomings of globalization is wrong. The problems with questionable efficiency benefits and sizable equity costs from some policies will not go away if we do not acknowledge them. Rather than shy away from inconvenient truths, designing policies so they deliver inclusive growth will be a more durable response than leaving matters to the trickle-down effects of growth (Guriev, Leipziger, Ostry 2017).

Trampolines and safety nets: Policies such as job counseling and retraining allow workers to bounce back from job loss: they help people adjust faster when economic shocks occur, reduce long unemployment spells, and hence keep the skills of workers from depreciating. While such programs already exist in many advanced economies, they deserve further study so that all can benefit from best practice. Safety-net programs have a role to play too. Governments can offer wage insurance for workers displaced into lower-paying jobs and offer employers wage subsidies for hiring displaced workers. Programs such as the U.S. earned income tax credit should be extended to further narrow income gaps while encouraging people to work (Obstfeld 2016).

Broader sharing of the benefits of the financial sector and financial globalization: We need "a financial system that is both more ethical and oriented more to the needs of the real economy—a financial system that serves society and not the other way round" (Lagarde 2015). Policies that broaden access to finance for the poor and middle class are needed to help them garner the benefits of foreign flows of capital. Increased capital mobility across borders has often fueled international tax competition and deprived governments of revenues: a "race to the bottom leaves everyone at the bottom" (Lagarde 2014). The lower revenue makes it harder for governments to finance trampoline policies and safety nets without inordinately high taxes on labor or regressive consumption taxes. Hence, we need international coordination against tax avoidance to prevent the bulk of globalization gains from accruing disproportionately to capital (Obstfeld 2016).

"Predistribution" and redistribution: Over the long haul, policies that improve access to good education and health care for all classes of society are

needed to provide better equality of opportunity, as argued forcefully by former IMF chief economist Raghuram Rajan in his 2011 book *Fault Lines*. Of course, improving access is neither easy nor an overnight fix. Hence, in the interim, such "predistribution" policies need to be complemented by redistribution: "more progressive tax and transfer policies must play a role in spreading globalization's economic benefits more broadly" (Obstfeld 2016).

Since the Great Recession, much attention has been given to macro-financial linkages and, more recently, to fears of secular stagnation in growth. Broadly speaking, our book makes the point that just as much attention needs to be devoted to macro-distributional linkages and to the secular exclusion of large parts of the population from the benefits of increased growth.

DATA APPENDIX

A majority of the data used in this book fall into one of two categories: (1) measures of inequality, or (2) measures of economic policies.

(1) The Gini coefficient or index measures the extent to which the distribution of income among individuals or households within an economy deviates from a perfectly equal distribution. We calculate Ginis for both market and net incomes, and use the difference between the market and net Ginis as a measure of redistribution. Data on Gini coefficients come from the Standardized World Income Inequality Database (SWIID). The SWIID attempts to maximize the comparability of income inequality data and expands coverage to the widest possible across time and countries. The SWIID uses—as inputs—data on inequality from multiple sources including UNU-WIDER World Income Inequality Database (WIID), the OECD Income Distribution Database (IDD), and others.

Top income shares are from the WIID. Labor share of income—the ratio of labor compensation to national income—is from the Penn World Tables.

(2) Measures of economic policies come from various sources, particularly from Ostry, Berg, and Kothari (2018).

A list of databases used is given below:

Barro and Lee educational attainment dataset
Chinn and Ito (2006)

Lane and Milesi-Ferretti (2007)
OECD statistics
Penn World Tables 7.1 and 9.0
Polity IV (2011)
Quinn (1997)
Standardized World Income Inequality Database (SWIID), (Solt 2009)
UNU-WIDER World Income Inequality Database (WIID)
World Bank's World Development Indicators (WDI)
World Wealth and Income Database (WID)

Indicator Name	Description	Data Source	Used in Chapter(s)
Age dependency ratio	The ratio of dependents—people younger than fifteen or older than sixty-four—to the working-age population (those ages fifteen to sixty-four). Data are shown as the proportion of dependents per one hundred working-age population.	World Bank's World Development Indicators (WDI)	2
Autocracy	A composite index of competitiveness of political participation, the regulation of participation, the openness and competitiveness of executive recruitment, and constraints on the chief executive.	Polity IV database	3
Average years of total schooling	Average years of primary and secondary schooling.	Barro and Lee educational attainment dataset (version 1.2)	4, 9
Capital account liberalization	A measure that adds up how many restrictions have been in place in different countries and how these restrictions have been relaxed or tightened over the years. The index is available for 182 countries, in many but not all cases from 1970 to 2010, and it ranges from −2 (more restricted capital account) to 2.5 (less restricted).	Chinn and Ito (2006)	2, 4, 5

Indicator Name	Description	Data Source	Used in Chapter(s)
Capital account reforms	Indicators measuring the intensity of legal restrictions on residents' and nonresidents' ability to move capital into and out of a country. Index originally coded from 0 (fully repressed) to 100 (fully liberalized).	Based on the methodology in Quinn (1997) and Quinn and Toyoda (2008), drawing on information contained in the Fund's AREAER.	4, 5
Chief executive party orientation	A discrete variable for left-, center-, right-wing government. The variable is taken from the Database of Political Institutions and assumes value 0 for left-wing governments, 1 for center-wing governments, and 2 for right-wing governments.	World Bank's Database of Political Institutions	2
Collective bargaining index	Higher values of the index indicate less centralized bargaining systems (i.e., more liberalized labor markets).	World Economic Forum, Global Competitiveness Report	4
Currency, debt and financial crises	Database indicating the start and end year of financial crisis by country. Please see Laeven and Valencia (2010) for more details on the criteria.	Laeven and Valencia (2010), "Resolution of Banking Crises: The Good, the Bad, and the Ugly." IMF Working Paper WP/10/146	5
Current account reforms	An indicator of how compliant a government is with its obligations under the IMF's Article VIII requiring members to keep their exchange systems free from restrictions on payments and transfers for current international transactions	Based on the methodology in Quinn (1997) and Quinn and Toyoda (2008), drawing on information contained in the Fund's AREAER	4, 5

(continued)

Indicator Name	Description	Data Source	Used in Chapter(s)
Current transfers received by households (% of GDP)	The sum of all cash payments received by households from governments as a percent of GDP	OECD National Accounts database (2012)	9
Debt liabilities to GDP	See Lane and Milesi-Ferretti (2007) for more details.	Updated and extended version of the Lane and Milesi-Ferretti (2007) dataset covering 1970–2010	7
Domestic finance liberalization	Credit market freedom indictor (ownership of banks), based on the percentage of bank deposits held in privately owned banks.	Fraser Institute's EFW (Economic Freedom of the World) database	2
Domestic financial liberalization (including subindices securities market and banking)	Captures the degree of controls and competition in the banking system (extent of interest rate and credit controls, competition restrictions, and public ownership) as well as restrictions on the development of local securities markets (bonds and equities).	Abiad et al. (2008), following the methodology in Abiad and Mody (2005), based on various IMF reports and working papers, central bank websites, and others.	4
EU KLEMS	Basic output, input, and productivity data for thirty-four industries and eight aggregates according to the ISIC Rev. 4 industry classification.	www.euklems.net	5
Exchange rate competitiveness	Measured as a deviation from purchasing power parity, after adjusting for per capita income (i.e., the residuals of cross-sectional regressions of price levels on PPP GDP).	Berg and Ostry (2017). "Inequality and Unsustainable Growth: Two Sides of the Same Coin?" *IMF Economic Review*, 65(4), 792–815	3

Indicator Name	Description	Data Source	Used in Chapter(s)
External debt	Debt owed to foreign creditors.	Updated and extended version of dataset constructed by Lane and Milesi-Ferretti (2007)	3
External financial dependence	constructed for each industry as the median across all U.S. firms in a given industry of the ratio of total capital expenditures minus current cash flow to total capital expenditures.	Rajan and Zingales (1998)	5
Foreign direct investment (FDI)	Foreign direct investment, that is, investments made in a given country by foreign entities.	Updated and extended version of dataset constructed by Lane and Milesi-Ferretti (2007)	3
Fertility rate	Total fertility rate represents the number of children that would be born to a woman if she were to live to the end of her childbearing years and bear children in accordance with age-specific fertility rates of the specified year.	World Bank's World Development Indicators (WDI)	2
Financial deepening	Credit to GDP ratio.	The Global Financial Inclusion database (Global Findex) developed by Demirguc-Kunt and others (2015)	5
Fiscal consolidation episodes	The measure of fiscal consolidation constructed by the authors is based on a narrative approach and focuses on policy actions—tax hikes and/or spending cuts—taken by governments with the intent of reducing the budget deficit.	A New Action-Based Dataset of Fiscal Consolidation by DeVries et al. (2011)	6

(continued)

Indicator Name	Description	Data Source	Used in Chapter(s)
Fiscal policy shock	The database contains information on 173 episodes of fiscal consolidation for seventeen OECD economies (Australia, Austria, Belgium, Canada, Denmark, Finland, France, Germany, Ireland, Italy, Japan, Netherlands, Portugal, Spain, Sweden, the United Kingdom, and the United States) during 1978–2009. The magnitude of the fiscal consolidation episode ranges between 0.1 and about 5 percent of GDP, with an average of about 1 percent GDP.	DeVries et al. (2011)	6
GDP	Gross domestic Product	Penn World Tables, version 7.1	7
GDP per capita	Real GDP per capita based on constant 2011 national prices (in 2011 US$).	Penn World Tables, version 9.0. and 7.1	1, 3, 4, 7
GDP per capita (by income decile)	A measure of per capita GDP by income decile (1–10) where the poorest 10th of the population is decile 1 and the richest is decile 10.	U.S. Bureau of Economic Analysis, NIPA Table 7.1.	1
Gini of net and market incomes	The Gini index measures the extent to which the distribution of income among individuals or households within an economy deviates from a perfectly equal distribution where market Gini is the measure before transfers and net Gini is after transfers.	UNU-WIDER, World Income Inequality Database (WIID3c), September 2015	2, 3
Gini of market and net incomes	The Gini index measures the extent to which the distribution of income among individuals or households within an economy deviates from a perfectly equal distribution where market Gini is the measure before taxes and transfers and net Gini is after taxes and transfers.	Solt (2009)	2, 4, 6, 7

Indicator Name	Description	Data Source	Used in Chapter(s)
Government size	Government expenditure as share of GDP.	World Bank's World Development Indicators (WDI)	2, 4
Growth spell	Period of growth between upbreak and downbreak.	Beerg and Ostry (2017)	3
Income shares	The amount of income going to the top or bottom percentiles of the income distribution.	The World Wealth and Income Database	1
Inflation	The increase in the general level of prices of goods and services in a country, measured as annual percent change.	Consensus Forecasts	7
Interest rate	Short-term deposit rate.	IMF World Economic Outlook	7
Investment	PPP of investment over exchange rate.	Penn World Tables, version 7.1	4, 7
Labor share of income	The level of income going to labor (as opposed to capital) as a share of all income.	Penn World Tables, version 9.0.	2, 5, 6, 7, 8
Law and order	This index assesses the impartiality of the legal system and the popular observance of the law.	Political Risk Service Group, International Country Risk Guide data	4
Liberalized trade	Measured with the Wacziarg and Welch (2007) dichotomous variable that takes a value of 1 when trade has been liberalized and 0 otherwise.	Wacziarg, Romain and Karen Horn Welch. "Trade Liberalization and Growth: New Evidence." World Bank Economic Review 22, 2 (June 2008): 187–231	3
Mortality rate	Under-five mortality rate is the probability per 1,000 that a newborn baby will die before reaching age five, if subject to age-specific mortality rates of the specified year.	World Bank's World Development Indicators (WDI)	2

(continued)

Indicator Name	Description	Data Source	Used in Chapter(s)
Net income by decile	Income after taxes and transfers.	UNU-WIDER World Income Inequality Database (WIID3c), September 2015	2
Network reforms	Index measures the extent of competition and quality of regulations in the telecommunications and electricity sectors.	Ostry Berg and Kothari (2018)	4
Political institutions (polity2)	Polity IV Project, Political Regime Characteristics and Transitions, 1800–2012, annual, cross-national, time-series and polity-case formats coding democratic and autocratic "patterns of authority" and regime changes in all independent countries with total population greater than 500,000.	Polity IV (2011)	3
Population density	Midyear population divided by land area in square kilometers.	World Bank's World Development Indicators (WDI)	2
Population growth	Annual population growth rate for year t is the exponential rate of growth of midyear population from year $t - 1$ to t, expressed as a percentage.	World Bank's World Development Indicators (WDI)	2
Redistribution	The difference between market and net Gini.	Solt (2009)	2
Regulation reforms	An episode where the annual change in a composite measure of credit, product, and labor market regulation exceeds by two standard deviations the average annual change over all observations. Higher values of the indicators indicate more open and competitive markets.	Fraser Institute's Economic Freedom of the World database	5
Wage income (% in GDP)	The share of total income from wages in overall GDP	OECD	6

Indicator Name	Description	Data Source	Used in Chapter(s)
Social expenditure (% of GDP)	Social expenditure comprises cash benefits, direct in-kind provision of goods and services, and tax breaks with social purposes. To be considered "social," programs have to involve either redistribution of resources across households or compulsory participation.	OECD National Accounts database (2012)	9
Social security benefits paid by general government (% of GDP)	Total cash and in-kind provision of goods and services provided by governments for social purposes as percent of GDP.	OECD National Accounts database (2012)	9
Structural break	A statistically significant change in the per capita real GDP growth rate that persists for at least eight years.	Berg and Ostry (2017)	3
Subsidies (% of GDP)	Total government subsidies as percent of GDP.	OECD National Accounts database (2012)	9
Subsidies and other transfers (% of expense)	Subsidies, grants, and other social benefits include all unrequited, nonrepayable transfers on current account to private and public enterprises; grants to foreign governments, international organizations, and other government units; and social security, social assistance benefits, and employer social benefits in cash and in-kind.	World Bank World Development Indicators (2013)	9
Tariff barriers	A weighted average tariff rate (based on most favored nation tariffs) normalized to lie between 0 and 1, with higher values of the index implying lower tariff levels (more openness).	Quinn (1997). The index draws on information from the IMF's AREAER.	4

(continued)

Indicator Name	Description	Data Source	Used in Chapter(s)
Tax revenue (% of GDP)	Tax revenue refers to compulsory transfers to the central government for public purposes. Certain compulsory transfers such as fines, penalties, and most social security contributions are excluded. Refunds and corrections of erroneously collected tax revenue are treated as negative revenue.	World Bank World Development Indicators (2013)	9
Technological progress	The share of ICT capital in total capital stock.	OECD	2, 5
Terms of trade	Terms of trade of goods, in U.S. dollars.	IMF World Economic Outlook	3
Top income shares	The share of incomes going to the very top 0.1 percent, 1 percent, or 10 percent.	World Top Incomes Databases (WTID) constructed by Facundo Alvaredo, Tony Atkinson, Thomas Piketty, Emmanuel Saez, and Gabriel Zucman. Link to the data: www.wid.world	5, 7
Total tax revenue (% of GDP)	Total tax revenue as a percentage of GDP indicates the share of a country's output that is collected by the government through taxes. It can be regarded as one measure of the degree to which the government controls the economy's resources.	OECD National Accounts database (2012)	9
Trade openness	The share of exports and imports in GDP.	Penn World Tables, version 7.1	2
Unemployment rate	Number of unemployed as percent of labor force.	OECD Analytical database	6
World KLEMS	Data on output, inputs, and productivity is available at the industry-level.	www.worldklems.net	5

TECHNICAL APPENDIX

OVERVIEW OF TECHNICAL WORK

The empirical analysis in this book is concerned with (1) the drivers of inequality, particularly economic policies; (2) efficiency/equity trade-off, which requires that we also look at drivers of growth; and (3) the links among inequality, growth, and redistribution (the difference between gross and net measures of inequality). Much of our empirical work therefore takes the form of regressions where either inequality or growth is the dependent variable and various economic policies are among the independent variables. In the case of (3), the dependent variable is growth and the main independent variables of interest are inequality and redistribution. The exact form of the regressions varies across chapters depending on the particular needs of the chapter. In this Technical Appendix, we first summarize the main empirical methods used in each chapter, and then take a detailed look at the specific regressions and results that underlie the figures in the book.

In chapter 2, we try to determine the robust drivers of inequality. The empirical framework used is the following:

$$I_{i,t:t+5} = \alpha_i + \gamma_t + bX_{i,t:t+5} + \varepsilon_{i,t:t+5}$$

where I denotes inequality over the period [t, t+5], measured by the Gini index of market (net) inequality; α_i and γ_t are country and time fixed effects, respectively; and X is a set of drivers or determinants. The equation is estimated using weighted-average least squares, which is a standard way of establishing which determinants are truly important in explaining the behavior of the dependent variable.

Chapter 3 establishes a key result of the book: inequality raises the odds that a growth spell will come to an end. A lot of the technical work in this chapter is therefore concerned with measuring growth spells by using statistical procedures to identify structural breaks in growth. The other technical exercise in this chapter is modeling how the hazard rate—the probability that a spell will end—depends on factors such as inequality. Chapter 9 uses similar methods because it too is concerned in part with determinants of the duration of growth spell, in particular whether redistribution matters. This chapter also has regressions where the dependent variable is growth (rather than the duration of growth spells) and the independent variables include inequality and measures of redistribution.

Chapter 4 studies how various structural reforms affect inequality and growth (taking into account the impact of inequality itself on growth, as established in chapter 3). To assess the direct effect of reforms and inequality on growth, we use standard dynamic (convergence) growth regressions of the form

$$\frac{y_{i,t} - y_{i,t-4}}{5} = \beta_1 \, y_{i,t-4} + \gamma_1 \, \overline{SR}_{i,t}^{\,j} + \gamma_2 \, \overline{Ineq}_{i,t} + \alpha_1 \overline{X}_{i,t} + \mu_i + \mu_t + \epsilon_{i,t}$$

where $y_{i,t}$ is the log of per capita GDP of country i at time t, $\overline{SR}_{i,t}^{\,j}$ is the average of the structural reform indicator between time t–4 and t, $\overline{Ineq}_{i,t}$ is the level of inequality averaged between time t–4 and t, while $\overline{X}_{i,t}$ represents other controls also averaged between t–4 and t. Analogous inequality convergence regressions are run to assess reforms' effects on inequality:

$$\frac{Gini_{i,t} - Gini_{i,t-4}}{5} = \beta_2 \, Gini_{i,t-4} + \gamma_3 \, \overline{SR}_{i,t}^{\,j} + \alpha_2 \overline{X}_{i,t} + \mu_i + \mu_t + \epsilon_{i,t}$$

where $Gini_{i,t}$ is the Gini coefficient for market inequality of country i at time t, $\overline{SR}_{i,t}^{\,j}$ is the average of the structural reform indicator between time t–4 and t, while $\overline{X}_{i,t}$ represents other controls also averaged between t–4 and t.

Chapters 5, 6, 7 are detailed analyses of the impact of specific policies—capital account liberalization, fiscal consolidation, and monetary policies, respectively—on inequality and output. In chapter 5, the autoregressive distributed lag model is used to assess the dynamic response of inequality in the aftermath of an episode of capital account liberalization. The equation is:

$$g_{it} = a_i + \gamma_t + \sum_{k=1}^{l} \beta_k g_{i,t-k} + \sum_{j=0}^{l} \delta_k D_{i,t-k} + \sum_{k=1}^{l} \vartheta_k X_{i,t-k} + \varepsilon_{it}$$

where the dependent variable g_{it} is the annual change in the log of output (or the Gini coefficient) and D is the index of capital account liberalization. Full sets of country-fixed and time-fixed effects denoted by a_i and γ_t are included. Second, impulse-response functions are used to describe the response of output and inequality to capital account liberalization. The shape of these response functions depends on the value of the δ and β coefficients. For instance, the simultaneous response is δ_0, and the one-year-ahead cumulative response is $\delta_0 + (\delta_1 + \beta_0 \delta_0)$.

In chapters 6 and 7, a local projections method is used to assess the response of inequality and growth to episodes of fiscal consolidation. The equation is:

$$g_{it} = \alpha_i^k + \vartheta_t^k + \beta^k MP_{i,t} + \pi^k X_{i,t} + \varepsilon_{i,t}^k$$

where the dependent variable g_{it} is the annual change in the log of output or the change in some measure of inequality; $MP_{i,t}$ is either the fiscal consolidation episode (in chapter 6) or the exogenous monetary policy shock (in chapter 7). Full sets of country-fixed and time-fixed effects denoted by α_i and ϑ_t are included. The equation is estimated for each future period k, and the impulse response functions and confidence intervals are computed using the estimated coefficients β^k and associated standard errors.

Chapter 8 departs from the norm—it is based on a theoretical model rather than econometric estimation.

The rest of this appendix explains the detailed procedure for each figure where econometric work is involved in generating the results shown.

EXPLANATIONS FOR INDIVIDUAL FIGURES

Figure 2.8

The empirical framework used to establish the robust determinants of inequality is the following:

$$I_{i,t:t+5} = \alpha_i + \gamma_t + bX_{i,t:t+5} + \varepsilon_{i,t:t+5} \qquad (T1)$$

where I denotes inequality over the period $[t, t+5]$, measured by the Gini index of market (net) inequality; α_i and γ_t are country- and time-fixed effects, respectively; and X is a set of determinants, which includes:

➤ Structural factors: Mortality rates; share of industry in GDP.

➤ Trends: Trade openness (the share of exports and imports in GDP); technological progress (the share of ICT capital in total capital stock).

➤ Policy: Government size (government expenditure as share of GDP); capital account liberalization (Chinn-Ito measure); domestic finance liberalization (Ostry, Prati, and Spilimbergo [2009] reform indicator).

➤ Others: Chief executive party orientation—a discrete variable for left-, center-, right-wing government; currency, debt, and financial crises.

Equation (T1) is estimated using weighted-average least squares on five-year non-overlapping panels for an unbalanced sample of ninety countries over the period 1980–2013. The procedure is implemented after first de-meaning the dependent variable and all determinants by country- and time-fixed effects.

■ ■ ■

Figures 3.1, 3.2, and 3.3

We apply a variant of a procedure proposed by Bai and Perron (1998, 2003) for testing for multiple structural breaks in time series when both the total number and the location of breaks are unknown. Our approach differs from the Bai-Perron approach in that it uses sample-specific critical values that take into account heteroskedasticity and small sample size as opposed to asymptotic critical values; and in that it extends Bai and Perron's algorithm for sequential testing of structural breaks, as described below.

At the outset, we must decide on the minimum interstitiary period: the minimum number of years, h, between breaks. Given a sample size T, the interstitiary period h will determine the maximum number of breaks, m, for each country: $m = int(T / h) - 1$. For example, if $T = 50$ and $h = 8$, then $m = int(6.25) - 1 = 5$. In Bai and Perron's terminology, the ratio h/T is referred to as the "trimming factor." Because T equals 35 to 55 observations, our choices of h imply trimming factors between 10 percent and 20 percent.

Imposing a long interstitiary period means that we could be missing true breaks that are less than h periods away from each other, or from the beginning or end of the sample period. However, allowing a short interstitiary period implies that some structural break tests may have to be undertaken on data subsamples containing as few as $2h + 1$ observations. In these circumstances, the size of the test may no longer be reliable, and the power to reject the null hypothesis of no structural break on the subsample may be low. Moreover, we hypothesize that breaks at shorter frequencies may have different determinants, and in particular may embody cyclical factors that we are less interested in here. Balancing these factors, we set h either equal to 8 or to 5.

We next employ an algorithm that sequentially tests for the presence of up to m breaks in the GDP growth series. The first step is to test for the null hypothesis of zero structural breaks against the alternative of one *or more* structural breaks (up to the preset maximum m). The location of potential breaks is decided by minimizing the sum of squared residuals between the actual data and the average growth rate before and after the break. Critical values are generated through Monte Carlo simulations, using bootstrapped residuals that take into account the properties of the actual time series (that is, sample size and variance).

In the event that the null hypothesis of zero structural breaks is rejected, we next examine the null of exactly one break, the location of which is again optimally chosen. This is tested by applying the same test as before—that is, testing the null of zero breaks against one or more breaks—on the *subsamples* to the right and left of the hypothesized break (up to the maximum number of breaks that the subsample length will allow given the interstitiary period). If *any* of the tests on the subsamples rejects, we move to testing the null of exactly two breaks, by testing for zero against one or more breaks on the three subsamples on the right, left, and in between the optimally chosen two breaks, and so on. The procedure ends when the hypothesis of l structural breaks can no longer be rejected against the alternative of more than l breaks.

MEASURING GROWTH SPELLS

The period following a growth upbreak can be thought of as a growth spell: a time period of higher growth than before, ending either with a downbreak or with the end of the sample. However, it is sometimes the case (after periods of very high growth) that high growth continues, albeit at a lower level. In this case, one would not want to say that a growth spell has ended. Conversely, it is sometime the case that an upbreak follows a period of sharply negative growth, leading to a period in which growth is still negative (or positive but very small). In this case, one would not want to say that a growth spell is underway. In short, if the objective is to understand the determinants of *desirable* growth spells, the statistical criteria discussed in the previous section need to be supplemented by an economic criterion. We hence define growth spells as periods of time

> ➢ *beginning* with a statistical upbreak followed by a period of *at least g* percent average growth, and
> ➢ *ending* either with a statistical downbreak followed by a period of *less than g* percent average growth (*complete* growth spells) or with the end of the sample (*incomplete* growth spells).

Because growth in our definition means per capita income growth, growth of as low as 2 percent might be considered a reasonable threshold. We used $g = 2$, $g = 2.5$, and $g = 3$, with similar results, and focus on the $g = 2$ case.

Figure 3.1 illustrates the procedure described above for six country cases and Figure 3.2 provides summary statistics on the properties of growth spells. Figure 3.3 shows how inequality is inversely related to the duration of growth spells.

Figure 3.4

Let t denote analysis time (time since growth accelerated) and T denote duration (the length of a growth spell), a random variable. Thus $t = 1$ denotes the first year in a growth spell, $t < 1$ years prior to the beginning of the spell. $X(t)$ is a vector of random variables that may influence the probability that a growth spell ends (also a random variable); x_t is the realization of $X(t)$ at time t; and z is a vector of non-time-varying variables that may also have an impact on the length of a growth spell. z could contain realizations of $X(t)$

before the beginning of a growth spell (i.e., x_t, $t < 1$) and also variables that have no time dimension at all (e.g., geographical variables). We want to estimate the effect of $X(t)$ and z of interest on T.

Duration is usually modeled by parameterizing the *hazard rate*—the conditional probability that the spell will end in the next period—and estimating the relevant parameters using maximum likelihood. In the presence of both time-varying and time-invariant covariates, the hazard rate can be defined as (assuming continuous time):

$$\lambda[t, X(t), z] = \lim_{h \to 0} \frac{P[t \leq T < t+h \mid T \geq t, X(t+h), z]}{h} = \frac{f(t \mid x_t, z)}{1 - F(t \mid x_t, z)}$$

(T2)

where $F(t \mid x_t, z)$ and $f(t \mid x_t, z)$ are the c.d.f. and density function of T, respectively, conditioning on z and the realization of X at time t. The most popular approach to estimating equation (T2) is to assume a proportional hazard model—in effect, an assumption that the time dependence of λ, called the "baseline hazard," is multiplicatively separable from its dependence on $[X(t), z]$—and to parameterize it by assuming that the relationship between λ and $[X(t), z]$ is log–linear, and that the baseline hazard takes a particular functional form:

$$\lambda(t) = g[X(t), z]\lambda_0(t) = \exp\{\beta[X(t), z]\}\lambda_0(t)$$

(T3)

where $\lambda_0(t)$ is assumed to obey a specific distribution whose parameters can be estimated along with the coefficient vector β. We have used as a baseline specification the assumption that $\lambda_0(t)$ follows a Weibull distribution, that is, $\lambda_0(t) = pt^{p-1}$. The parameter P, which is estimated, determines whether duration dependence is positive ($p > 1$) or negative.

We start by characterizing the unconditional hazard rate, or the probability that a spell will end after a given number of years, conditional only on the fact that it has already lasted up to that point. We then examine the role of external shocks, then of institutions and variables related to social conflict (income distribution and ethnic heterogeneity), and then of a variety of other policy-related indicators, using some of the previous variables as controls. Results are presented in table T1 through table T4.

TABLE T1: Duration Regressions—Institutions

Model	Variable	Eight-year minimum spell		Five-year minimum spell	
		Time ratio	*p* value	Time ratio	*p* value
1	Polity 2 (Polity IV database) Initial level	*1.12*	*0.10*	*1.10*	*0.01*
	Change within spell	*1.11*	*0.07*	*1.10*	*0.02*
	Spells/failures	46/17		66/35	
2	Polity 2 (Polity IV database)	*1.12*	*0.04*	*1.12*	*0.00*
	Spells/failures	51/17		72/37	
3	Democracy (Polity IV database)	*1.17*	*0.11*	*1.22*	*0.00*
	Spells/failures	51/17		72/37	
4	Autocracy (Polity IV database)	*0.77*	*0.01*	*0.80*	*0.00*
	Spells/failures	51/17		72/37	
5	Executive recruitment (Polity IV database)	*1.42*	*0.02*	*1.35*	*0.00*
	Spells/failures	51/17		72/37	
6	Executive constraints (Polity IV database)	*1.35*	*0.07*	*1.42*	*0.00*
	Spells/failures	51/17		72/37	
7	Political competition (Polity IV database)	*1.26*	*0.05*	*1.23*	*0.00*
	Spells/failures	51/17		72/37	
8	Investment profile (ICRG)	*1.64*	*0.29*	*1.36*	*0.08*
	Spells/failures	34/4		46/16	

TABLE T2: Duration Regressions—Inequality and Fractionalization

Model	Variable	Eight-year minimum spell		Five-year minimum spell	
		Time ratio	*p* value	Time ratio	*p* value
1	Inequality (Gini coefficient) Initial level	*0.87*	*0.02*	*0.85*	*0.00*
	Change within spell	1.08	0.31	0.94	0.28
	Spells/failures	22/6		32/14	
2	Inequality (Gini coefficient)	*0.89*	*0.03*	*0.89*	*0.00*
	Spells/failures	31/11		45/21	
3	Ethnic fractionalization (Alesina, Spolaore, and Wacziarg 2005)	0.99	0.41	0.99	0.40
	Spells/failures	56/19		86/45	
4	Ethnic fractionalization (Alesina , Spolaore, and Wacziarg 2005)	*0.96*	*0.02*	*0.98*	*0.10*
	Inequality (Gini coefficient)	*0.91*	*0.03*	*0.89*	*0.00*
	Spells/failures	31/11		45/21	

TABLE T3: Duration Regressions—Globalization

Model	Variable	Eight-year minimum spell		Five-year minimum spell	
		Time ratio	*p* value	Time ratio	*p* value
	Trade liberalization (Wacziarg–Welch dummy variable)				
1	Initial level	2.83	0.21	*6.56*	*0.00*
	Change within spell	*6.76*	*0.02*	*7.88*	*0.00*
	Spells/failures	38/16		61/33	
	Trade openness (based on PWT data, adjusted for structural characteristics)				
2	Initial level	*1.04*	*0.03*	1.01	0.33
	Change within spell	*1.04*	*0.01*	1.01	0.15
	Spells/failures	51/15		76/35	
	Financial integration (sum of external assets and liabilities)				
3	Initial level	1.01	0.54	1.00	0.87
	Change within spell	1.01	0.52	1.00	0.60
	Spells/failures	29/7		40/18	
	External debt liabilities				
4	Initial level	1.00	0.90	1.00	0.57
	Change within spell	1.00	0.92	1.00	0.18
	Spells/failures	29/7		40/18	
	FDI liabilities				
5	Initial level	1.00	0.99	1.03	0.27
	Change within spell	1.05	0.22	*1.11*	*0.02*
	Spells/failures	29/7		40/18	

TABLE T4: Duration Regressions—Macroeconomic Volatility

Model	Variable	Eight-year minimum spell		Five-year minimum spell	
		Time ratio	p value	Time ratio	p value
1	Log (1 + inflation)				
	Initial level	1.00	0.94	1.01	0.58
	Change within spell	0.97	0.60	*0.99*	*0.02*
	Spells/failures	54/9		82/43	
2	Log (1 + depreciation in the parallel exchange rate)				
	Initial level	*0.94*	*0.02*	0.99	0.12
	Change within spell	*0.96*	*0.06*	0.99	*0.10*
	Spells/failures	23/9		34/18	
3	Log (1 + moderate inflation)				
	Initial level	0.96	0.45	*0.91*	*0.0*
	Change within spell	0.98	0.64	*0.94*	*0.02*
	Spells/failures	49/19		76/42	
4	Average growth within spell	*0.84*	*0.01*	*0.86*	*0.00*
	Spells/failures	57/19		88/46	
5	Log (1 + inflation)				
	Initial level	1.01	0.84	1.00	0.7
	Change within spell	0.98	060	*0.99*	*0.01*
	Average growth within spell	*0.81*	*0.01*	*0.86*	*0.00*
	Spells/failures	54/19		82/43	
6	Log (1 + depreciation in the parallel exchange rate)				
	Initial level	0.98	0.36	*0.99*	*0.06*
	Change within spell	*0.97*	*0.04*	*0.98*	*0.01*
	Average growth within spell	*0.64*	*0.00*	*0.85*	*0.00*
	Spells/failures	23/9		34/18	
7	Debt/GDP change within spell				
	Average growth within spell	0.97	0.20	*0.98*	*0.05*
	Log (1 + inflation)	*0.67*	*0.09*	*0.81*	*0.02*
	Initial level	1.01	0.88	1.00	0.93
	Change within spell	1.00	0.96	*0.99*	*0.02*
	Spells/failures	33/8		44/18	

Figures 4.3, 4.4, 4.5, and 4.6

To assess the direct and indirect effect of reforms on the level of per capita GDP, we run separate regressions with growth and inequality as dependent variables. We include our different structural reform variables on the right-hand side (one variable at a time). All regressions use five-year averaged data.

To assess the direct effect of reforms and inequality on growth, we use standard dynamic (convergence) growth regressions of the form

$$\frac{y_{i,t} - y_{i,t-4}}{5} = \beta_1\, y_{i,t-4} + \gamma_1\, \overline{SR}_{i,t}^{\,j} + \gamma_2 \overline{Ineq}_{i,t} + \alpha_1 \overline{X}_{i,t} + \mu_i + \mu_t + \epsilon_{i,t} \qquad (T4)$$

where $y_{i,t}$ is the log of per capita GDP of country i at time t, $\overline{SR}_{i,t}^{\,j}$ is the average of the structural reform indicator between time $t-4$ and t, $\overline{Ineq}_{i,t}$ is the level of inequality averaged between time $t-4$ and t, while $\overline{X}_{i,t}$ represents other controls also averaged between $t-4$ and t. Following Ostry, Berg, and Tsanga-rides (2014), in our baseline specification we include net inequality as a control variable. We do robustness checks in which the log of investment and the log of total education are also included as controls. A negative value for β_1 implies convergence. The coefficients of interest are γ_1, which captures the direct effect of reform on growth, and γ_2 which captures the effect of inequality on growth.

Analogous inequality convergence regressions are run to assess reforms' effects on inequality. The equation is:

$$\frac{Gini_{i,t} - Gini_{i,t-4}}{5} = \beta_2\, Gini_{i,t-4} + \gamma_3\, \overline{SR}_{i,t}^{\,j} + \alpha_2 \overline{X}_{i,t} + \mu_i + \mu_t + \epsilon_{i,t} \qquad (T5)$$

where $Gini_{i,t}$ is the Gini coefficient for market inequality of country i at time t, $\overline{SR}_{i,t}^{\,j}$ is the average of the structural reform indicator between time $t-4$ and t, while $\overline{X}_{i,t}$ represents other controls also averaged between $t-4$ and t. The coefficient of interest is γ_3, as this tells us the impact effect of reforms on inequality.

We include the averaged growth rate of per capita GDP as one of the Xs in the inequality regression to allow for two-way causation between inequality and growth. In this specification, reforms affect only the *level* of inequality in the steady state. However, the presence of lagged inequality on the right-hand side allows for dynamic effects, with reforms impacting the Gini gradually over time.

All regressions are estimated using system generalized method of moments (GMM) to try to account for reverse causality, endogeneity, and dynamic panel bias. Standard errors are clustered at the country level. While it is natural to use system GMM techniques to estimate dynamic panel regressions, we also checked for robustness by estimating pooled OLS as well as fixed-effect regressions. The results for the effects of reform on growth are similar irrespective of the estimation method. For the inequality regression, pooled OLS gives broadly similar results to system GMM while the results are usually weaker for fixed effects, suggesting that cross-country variation is important for identifying the reform–inequality relation.

Note that we include the contemporaneous level of the structural reform and other control variables on the right-hand side but instrument these with lags to account for potential endogeneity. Using the reform index at the beginning of the period instead of the contemporaneous average yields broadly similar results for the inequality regressions, although the effect of reforms on growth is somewhat weaker.

Tables T5 through T11 report the regression results for domestic finance, tariff reforms, current account liberalization, capital account liberalization, networks reforms, collective bargaining reforms, and law and order, respectively. In each table, column (1) reports the results for the whole sample (for figure 4.3); column (4) reports the results for the subsample of low-income countries (LICs) and middle-income countries (MICs) (for figure 4.4).

TOTAL EFFECT

As discussed in the text, and shown in the tables, for a number of indicators we find that reforms increase inequality as well as growth. In chapter 3, we showed that higher levels of inequality may reduce growth. This raises the question: what is the total effect of reforms on growth? That is, after taking into account the higher inequality following reforms, how much lower is the effect of reforms on growth (and is it even positive)? To answer this question, we carry out some simple calculations by combining results from the separate growth and inequality regressions. First, consider the direct effect of reforms on the steady-state level of log of per capita GDP (holding inequality constant). From equation (T4), a change in the reform index from the median to the

TABLE T5: Domestic Finance Reforms—Growth-Equity Trade-off

Variables	(1) Growth All Countries	(2) Growth All Countries	(3) Inequality All Countries	(4) Growth LIC and MIC	(5) Growth LIC and MIC	(6) Inequality LIC and MIC
Domestic finance	0.0630*** (0.0146)	0.0478*** (0.0149)	0.0065* (0.0038)	0.0633** (0.0261)	0.0210 (0.0263)	0.0137** (0.0058)
Net inequality	−0.1505*** (0.0527)	−0.0782* (0.0425)		−0.1940** (0.0911)	−0.0042 (0.0909)	
Log (investment)		0.0410*** (0.0125)			0.0551*** (0.0089)	
Log (education)		0.0004 (0.0085)			0.0143 (0.0171)	
Lagged per capita GDP	−0.0126*** (0.0037)	−0.0129*** (0.0037)		−0.0130* (0.0072)	−0.0197** (0.0093)	
Growth of per capita GDP			−0.0378 (0.0234)			−0.0128 (0.0402)
Lagged inequality			−0.0484*** (0.0147)			−0.0482 (0.0343)
Effect of reforms (75–50 percentile)	0.35	0.25	1.57	0.35	0.09	3.32
Observations	444	427	392	271	254	225
No. of countries	74	70	74	49	45	49
No. of instruments	65	63	65	36	63	37
AR2	0.237	0.344	0.230	0.0567	0.365	0.133
Hansen	0.450	0.393	0.319	0.310	0.988	0.234

Note: Details of reform variable in appendix 1. First column reports results of a standard growth regression (equation T4). Column 2 adds additional controls to the growth regression. Column 3 reports results for the dynamic inequality regression (equation T5) with change in market inequality on the LHS. Columns 4 to 6 repeat the same regressions but for the restricted sample of LICs and MICs only. Row "Effect of reforms" reports the effect on per capita GDP (in percent) and inequality (in Gini points) in the long run (30 years) of moving the reform index from the median to the seventy-fifth percentile. All regressions include country- and time-fixed effects. Estimation done using system GMM. P-value of Hansen and AR2 test reported. Robust standard errors clustered at country level in parentheses *** $p < 0.01$, ** $p < 0.05$, * $p < 0.1$.

Source: Data on per capita GDP growth and investment from Penn World Tables 7.1. Total education from Barro and Lee (2012). Net and market inequality from SWIID 5.0.

TABLE T6: Tariff Reforms—Growth-Equity Trade-off

Variables	(1) Growth All Countries	(2) Growth All Countries	(3) Inequality All Countries	(4) Growth LIC and MIC	(5) Growth LIC and MIC	(6) Inequality LIC and MIC
Tariff reform	0.0385** (0.0158)	0.0395** (0.0167)	0.0065* (0.0038)	0.0198 (0.0164)	0.0352* (0.0197)	0.0041 (0.0061)
Net inequality	−0.1311** (0.0536)	−0.1059*** (0.0394)		−0.0770* (0.0438)	−0.0492 (0.0422)	
Log (investment)		0.0410*** (0.0071)			0.0265*** (0.0083)	
Log (education)		−0.0063 (0.0087)			0.0163 (0.0110)	
Lagged per capita GDP	−0.0052* (0.0027)	−0.0054* (0.0030)		−0.0012 (0.0036)	−0.0088** (0.0043)	
Growth of per capita GDP			−0.0383* (0.0222)			−0.0040 (0.0177)
Lagged inequality			−0.0172 (0.0155)			−0.0271 (0.0169)
Effect of reforms (75–50 percentile)	0.15	0.16	0.19	NA	0.13	1.26
Observations	685	635	601	467	418	392
No. of countries	130	112	123	98	81	92
No. of instruments	81	97	89	89	81	89
AR2	0.262	0.876	0.997	0.166	0.491	0.849
Hansen	0.327	0.116	0.612	0.614	0.243	0.890

Notes: Data on per capita GDP growth and investment from Penn World Tables 7.1. Total education from Barro and Lee (2012). Net and market inequality from SWIID 5.0. Details of reform variable in appendix 1. First column reports results of a standard growth regression (equation T4). Column 2 adds additional controls to the growth regression. Column 3 reports results for the dynamic inequality regression (equation T5) with change in market inequality on the LHS. Columns 4 to 6 repeat the same regressions but for the restricted sample of LICs and MICs only. Row "Effect of reforms" reports the effect on per capita GDP (in percent) and inequality (in Gini points) in the long run (30 years) of moving the reform index from the median to the seventy-fifth percentile. All regressions include country- and time-fixed effects. Estimation done using system GMM. *P*-value of Hansen and AR2 test reported. Robust standard errors clustered at country level in parentheses. ***p < 0.01, **p < 0.05, p < 0.1

TABLE T7: Current Account Liberalization—Growth-Equity Trade-off

Variables	(1) Growth All Countries	(2) Growth All Countries	(3) Inequality All Countries	(4) Growth LIC and MIC	(5) Growth LIC and MIC	(6) Inequality LIC and MIC
Current account restrictions	0.0240* (0.0131)	0.0241** (0.0116)	0.0096** (0.0038)	−0.0020 (0.0140)	0.0095 (0.0150)	0.0095*** (0.0034)
Net inequality	−0.2075*** (0.0544)	−0.1144*** (0.0383)		−0.1181** (0.0538)	−0.0678 (0.0508)	
Log (investment)		0.0337*** (0.0089)			0.0285*** (0.0094)	
Log (education)		−0.0128** (0.0063)			−0.0035 (0.0138)	
Lagged per capita GDP	−0.0082*** (0.0039)	−0.0070** (0.0027)		−0.0070 (0.0059)	−0.0081 (0.0067)	
Growth of per capita GDP			−0.0299 (0.0251)			0.0169 (0.0296)
Lagged inequality			−0.0298* (0.0157)			−0.0382** (0.0194)
Effect of reforms (75–50 percentile)	0.12	0.12	2.83	−0.01	0.05	2.40
Observations	741	714	589	458	432	348
No. of countries	100	93	96	68	62	65
No. of instruments	71	103	57	61	101	55
AR2	0.110	0.196	0.980	0.134	0.195	0.580
Hansen	0.0524	0.644	0.641	0.334	0.988	0.788

Notes: Data on per capita GDP growth and investment from Penn World Tables 7.1. Total education from Barro and Lee (2012). Net and market inequality from SWIID 5.0. Details of reform variable in appendix 1. First column reports results of a standard growth regression (equation 1. Column 2 adds additional controls to the growth regression. Column 3 reports results for the dynamic inequality regression (equation T5) with change in market inequality on the LHS. Columns 4 to 6 repeat the same regressions but for the restricted sample of LICs and MICs only. Row "Effect of reforms" reports the effect on pc GDP (in percent) and inequality (in Gini points) in the long run (30 years) of moving the reform index from the median to the seventy-fifth percentile. All regressions include country- and time-fixed effects. Estimation done using system GMM. *P*-value of Hansen and AR2 test reported. Robust standard errors clustered at country level in parentheses. ***p < 0.01, **p < 0.05, p < 0.1

TABLE T8: Capital Account Liberalization—Growth-Equity Trade-off

Variables	(1) Growth All Countries	(2) Growth All Countries	(3) Inequality All Countries	(4) Growth LIC and MIC	(5) Growth LIC and MIC	(6) Inequality LIC and MIC
Capital account restrictions	0.0181 (0.0113)	0.0144 (0.0103)	0.0075** (0.0027)	−0.0001 (0.0098)	−0.0035 (0.0094)	0.0065** (0.0030)
Net inequality	−0.1957*** (0.0541)	−0.0979*** (0.0357)		−0.0988* (0.0591)	−0.0408 (0.0676)	
Log (investment)		0.0348*** (0.0087)			0.0308** (0.0133)	
Log (education)		−0.0064 (0.0069)			−0.0101 (0.0121)	
Lagged per capita GDP	−0.0087*** (0.0037)	−0.0088*** (0.0029)		−0.0047 (0.0057)	−0.0057 (0.0051)	
Growth of per capita GDP			−0.0271 (0.0229)			0.0232 (0.0239)
Lagged inequality			−0.0436*** (0.0159)			−0.0592*** (0.0202)
Effect of reforms (75–50 percentile)	0.20	0.16	3.84	0.00	−0.03	2.62
Observations	741	714	589	458	432	348
No. of countries	100	93	96	68	62	65
No. of instruments	61	103	57	61	101	55
AR2	0.135	0.214	0.804	0.140	0.204	0.743
Hansen	0.139	0.632	0.561	0.624	1	0.625

Notes: Data on per capita GDP growth and investment from Penn World Tables 7.1. Total education from Barro and Lee (2012). Net and market inequality from SWIID 5.0. Details of reform variable in appendix 1. First column reports results of a standard growth regression (equation T1). Column 2 adds additional controls to the growth regression. Column 3 reports results for the dynamic inequality regression (equation T5) with change in market inequality on the LHS. Columns 4 to 6 repeat the same regressions but for the restricted sample of LICs and MICs only. Row "Effect of reforms" reports the effect on per capita GDP (in percent) and inequality (in Gini points) in the long run (30 years) of moving the reform index from the median to the seventy-fifth percentile. All regressions include country- and time-fixed effects. Estimation done using system GMM. *P*-value of Hansen and AR2 test reported. Robust standard errors clustered at country level in parentheses. ***p < 0.01, **p < 0.05, p < 0.1

TABLE T9: Networks Reforms—Growth-Equity Trade-off

Variables	(1) Growth All Countries	(2) Growth All Countries	(3) Inequality All Countries	(4) Growth LIC and MIC	(5) Growth LIC and MIC	(6) Inequality LIC and MIC
Networks reform	0.0029 (0.0136)	0.0040 (0.0104)	0.0031 (0.0022)	−0.0121 (0.0126)	−0.0022 (0.0135)	0.0064** (0.0029)
Net inequality	−0.0473 (0.0723)	−0.0516 (0.0413)		−0.0839 (0.0618)	−0.0496 (0.0536)	
Log (investment)		0.0389*** (0.0119)			0.0414** (0.0162)	
Log (education)		−0.0063 (0.0076)			−0.0061 (0.0184)	
Lagged per capita GDP	−0.0030 (0.00040)	−0.0047 (0.0047)		0.0074 (0.0081)	−0.0046 (0.0058)	
Growth of per capita GDP			−0.0232 (0.0227)			0.0008 (0.0335)
Lagged inequality			−0.0407*** (0.0119)			−0.0444*** (0.0167)
Effect of reforms (75–50 percentile)	−0.03	0.06	2.22	−0.21	−0.03	4.31
Observations	561	534	431	344	318	248
No. of countries	86	76	80	60	51	55
No. of instruments	85	89	48	45	83	42
AR2	0.180	0.234	0.624	0.127	0.203	0.138
Hansen	0.565	0.786	0.977	0.937	1	0.642

Notes: Data on per capita GDP growth and investment from Penn World Tables 7.1. Total education from Barro and Lee (2012). Net and market inequality from SWIID 5.0. Details of reform variable in appendix 1. First column reports results of a standard growth regression (equation T4). Column 2 adds additional controls to the growth regression. Column 3 reports results for the dynamic inequality regression (equation T5) with change in market inequality on the LHS. Columns 4 to 6 repeat the same regressions but for the restricted sample of LICs and MICs only. Row "Effect of reforms" reports the effect on per capita GDP (in percent) and inequality (in Gini points) in the long run (30 years) of moving the reform index from the median to the seventy-fifth percentile. All regressions include country- and time-fixed effects. Estimation done using system GMM. *P*-value of Hansen and AR2 test reported. Robust standard errors clustered at country level in parentheses. ***p < 0.01, **p < 0.05, p < 0.1

TABLE T10: Collective Bargaining Reforms—Growth-Equity Trade-off

Variables	(1) Growth All Countries	(2) Growth All Countries	(3) Inequality All Countries	(4) Growth LIC and MIC	(5) Growth LIC and MIC	(6) Inequality LIC and MIC
Current account restrictions	0.0404 (0.0249)	0.0118 (0.0250)	0.0027 (0.0060)	−0.0331 (0.0464)	−0.0011 (0.0396)	0.0116* (0.0063)
Net inequality	−0.0775 (0.0769)	−0.0563 (0.0370)		−0.0292 (0.1173)	0.0428 (0.0873)	
Log (investment)		0.0463*** (0.0135)			0.0275* (0.0166)	
Log (education)		0.0102 (0.0172)			−0.0027 (0.0453)	
Lagged per capita GDP	−0.0040 (0.0044)	−0.0076 (0.0052)		−0.0124* (0.0074)	−0.0010 (0.0143)	
Growth of per capita GDP			−0.0532* (0.0306)			−0.0344 (0.0320)
Lagged inequality			−0.0542*** (0.0149)			−0.0349** (0.0158)
Effect of reforms (75–50 percentile)	0.24	0.06	0.54	0.15	−0.01	3.19
Observations	451	439	431	220	208	212
No. of countries	96	90	95	66	60	65
No. of instruments	81	81	82	64	80	67
AR2	0.353	0.516	0.932	0.239	0.235	0.677
Hansen	0.717	0.733	0.926	0.996	1	1

Notes: Data on per capita GDP growth and investment from Penn World Tables 7.1. Total education from Barro and Lee (2012). Net and market inequality from SWIID 5.0. Details of reform variable in appendix 1. First column reports results of a standard growth regression (equation T4). Column 2 adds additional controls to the growth regression. Column 3 reports results for the dynamic inequality regression (equation T5) with change in market inequality on the LHS. Columns 4 to 6 repeat the same regressions but for the restricted sample of LICs and MICs only. Row "Effect of reforms" reports the effect on pc GDP (in percent) and inequality (in Gini points) in the long run (30 years) of moving the reform index from the median to the seventy-fifth percentile. All regressions include country- and time-fixed effects. Estimation done using system GMM. *P*-value of Hansen and AR2 test reported. Robust standard errors clustered at country level in parentheses. ***p < 0.01, **p < 0.05, *p < 0.1

TABLE T11: Law and Order—Growth-Equity Trade-off

Variables	(1) Growth All Countries	(2) Growth All Countries	(3) Inequality All Countries	(4) Growth LIC and MIC	(5) Growth LIC and MIC	(6) Inequality LIC and MIC
Law and order (ICRG)	0.0474** (0.0225)	0.0344 (0.0220)	0.0043 (0.0043)	0.0622*** (0.0215)	0.0462** (0.0185)	0.0023 (0.0067)
Net inequality	−0.0918 (0.0988)	−0.0616 (0.0480)		0.0187 (0.1021)	−0.0143 (0.0455)	
Log (investment)		0.0135* (0.0077)			0.0157** (0.0065)	
Log (education)		−0.0181 (0.0115)			0.0110 (0.0112)	
Lagged per capita GDP	−0.0080*** (0.0025)	−0.0136*** (0.0034)		−0.0033 (0.0042)	−0.0078 (0.0048)	
Growth of per capita GDP			−0.0761*** (0.0261)			−0.0114 (0.0404)
Lagged inequality			−0.0340** (0.0170)			−0.0232 (0.0164)
Effect of reforms (75–50 percentile)	0.39	0.23	1.73	0.61	0.38	1.14
Observations	471	435	426	324	289	283
No. of countries	108	97	104	77	67	74
No. of instruments	43	79	43	43	79	43
AR2	0.990	0.675	0.286	0.995	0.448	0.872
Hansen	0.0216	0.134	0.593	0.568	0.818	0.334

Notes: Data on per capita GDP growth and investment from Penn World Tables 7.1. Total education from Barro and Lee (2012). Net and market inequality from SWIID 5.0. Details of reform variable in appendix 1. First column reports results of a standard growth regression (equation T4). Column 2 adds additional controls to the growth regression. Column 3 reports results for the dynamic inequality regression (equation T5) with change in market inequality on the LHS. Columns 4 to 6 repeat the same regressions but for the restricted sample of LICs and MICs only. Row "Effect of reforms" reports the effect on per capita GDP (in percent) and inequality (in Gini points) in the long run (30 years) of moving the reform index from the median to the seventy-fifth percentile. All regressions include country- and time-fixed effects. Estimation done using system GMM. *P*-value of Hansen and AR2 test reported. Robust standard errors clustered at country level in parentheses. ***p < 0.01, **p < 0.05, p < 0.1

seventy-fifth percentile, denoted by ΔSR, results in a steady-state increase in log of per capita GDP of $\dfrac{\gamma_1 \Delta SR}{-\beta_1}$. Now, the same increase in the reform index leads to a steady-state increase in the Gini coefficient of $\dfrac{\gamma_3 \Delta SR}{-\beta_2}$ (from equation T5). The indirect effect of this increase in inequality on per capita GDP (in steady state) is therefore given by $\dfrac{\gamma_2}{-\beta_1} \dfrac{\gamma_3 \Delta SR}{-\beta_2}$, where γ_2 is the coefficient on inequality in the growth regression. Finally, the total effect on growth is the sum of direct and indirect effects. Figure 4.5 reports results for this calculation.

Figures 5.3, 5.4, and 5.5

To assess the impact of capital account liberalization, we follow the autoregressive distributed lag approach of Romer and Romer (2004), among others. This approach is particularly suited to assess the dynamic response of the variable of interest in the aftermath of a reform (a capital account liberalization episode in our case). The methodology consists of estimating a univariate autoregressive equation and deriving the associated impulse response functions:

$$g_{it} = a_i + \gamma_t + \sum_{k=1}^{l} \beta_k g_{i,t-k} + \sum_{j=0}^{l} \delta_k D_{i,t-k} + \sum_{k=1}^{l} \vartheta_k X_{i,t-k} + \varepsilon_{it} \qquad \text{(T6)}$$

where g is the annual change in the log of output (or the Gini coefficient, or the labor share); D is a dummy variable that is equal to 1 at the start of a capital account liberalization episode and zero otherwise; a_i are country-fixed effects included to control for unobserved cross-country heterogeneity; γ_t are time-fixed effects to control for global shocks. We include lagged output growth (inequality) to control for the normal dynamics of output (inequality). In addition, because the variables affecting output (inequality) in the short term are typically serially correlated, this also helps to control for various factors that may influence output (inequality).

Finally, because several types of economic reforms are often implemented simultaneously—this is particularly the case for current account and capital account reforms—we include in the baseline a set of other structural reform variables (X) to distinguish the effect of capital account liberalization episodes from others. Specifically, the set of reform variables included as controls are (1) current account reforms, defined as an episode where the annual change of the Quinn and Toyoda (2008) measure of current account openness exceeds by two standard deviations the average annual change over all observations, and (2) regulation reforms, defined as an episode where the annual change in a composite measure of credit, product, and labor market regulation exceeds by two standard deviations the average annual change over all observations.

Equation (T6) is estimated using OLS on an unbalanced panel of annual observations from 1970 to 2010 for 149 advanced and developing economies. While the presence of a lagged dependent variable and country-fixed effects may in principle bias the estimation of δ_j and β_j in small samples, the length of the time dimension mitigates this concern. The finite sample bias is in the order of $1/T$, where T in our sample is 41. Robustness checks using a two-step system-GMM estimator confirm the validity of the results. The number of lags chosen is two, but different lag lengths are tested as a robustness check.

Impulse response functions are used to describe the response of growth and inequality following a capital account liberalization episode. The shape of these response functions depends on the value of the δ and β coefficients. For instance, the simultaneous response is δ_0, the one-year-ahead cumulative response is $\delta_0 + (\delta_1 + \beta_0\delta_0)$. The confidence bands associated with the estimated impulse-response functions are obtained using the estimated standard errors of the estimated coefficients, based on clustered (at country-level) heteroskedasticity robust standard errors.

Figure 5.3 shows the impulse-response functions for growth and the Gini measure of inequality, figure 5.4 for the top income shares, and figure 5.5 for the labor share.

■ ■ ■

Figures 5.6 and 5.8

It is commonly argued that there are certain threshold levels of financial development (in particular the depth of the credit market) that an economy needs to attain before it can benefit from, and reduce the risks associated with, financial globalization. Capital account liberalization may allow better consumption smoothing and lower volatility for countries with strong financial institutions, but where institutions are weak and the access to credit is not inclusive, it may have limited output gains and further exacerbate inequality by increasing the bias in financial access in favor of people who are well off.

We re-examine this hypothesis by assessing whether the effect of capital account liberalization depends on the strength of financial institutions—depth and access to credit—and whether liberalization episodes are followed by crises. Specifically, we estimate the following equation:

$$g_{it} = a_i + \gamma_t + \sum_{j=1}^{l} \beta_j g_{i,t-j} + \sum_{j=1}^{l} \vartheta_j X_{i,t-j} + \sum_{j=0}^{l} \delta_j^- D_{i,t-j} G(z_{it})$$

$$+ \sum_{j=0}^{l} \delta_j^+ D_{i,t-j} [1 - G(z_{it})] + \varepsilon_{it} \tag{T7}$$

$$\text{with } G(z_{it}) = \frac{\exp(-\gamma z_{it})}{1 + \exp(-\gamma z_{it})}, \quad \gamma > 0,$$

in which z is an indicator of financial development, normalized to have zero mean and unit variance, and $G(z_{it})$ is the corresponding smooth transition function of the degree of financial development—in the case of crises the $G(.)$ function takes value one if episodes are followed by crises, zero otherwise. This approach is equivalent to the smooth transition autoregressive (STAR) model to assess nonlinear effects above/below a given threshold or regime. The main advantage of this approach relative to estimating structural vector autoregressive models for each regime is that it uses a larger number of observations to compute the impulse-response functions of only the dependent variables of interest, improving the stability and precision of the estimates. This estimation strategy can also more easily handle the potential correlation of the standard errors within countries, by clustering at the country level.

Figure 5.6 shows how the impact of capital account liberalization on growth and inequality depends on financial depth and inclusion and on the occurrence of crisis. Figure 5.8 shows how the impact on inequality depends on financial depth and inclusion in the case of LICs.

Figures 6.3, 6.4, and 6.5

To assess the distributional impact of fiscal consolidation episodes over the short and medium term, the paper follows the method proposed by Jordà (2005), which consists of estimating the dynamic change in inequality in the aftermath of fiscal adjustment episodes. Specifically, for each future year k the following equation has been estimated on annual data:

$$G_{i,t+k} - G_{i,t} = \alpha_i^k + \text{Time}_t^k + \sum_{j=1}^{l} \gamma_j^k \Delta G_{i,t-j} + \beta_k D_{i,t} + \varepsilon_{i,t}^k \qquad \text{(T8)}$$

with $k = 1 \ldots 8$, where G represents our measure of inequality (proxied by the Gini coefficient for disposable income); $D_{i,t}$ is a dummy variable that takes the value equal to 1 for the starting date of a consolidation episode in country i at time t and 0 otherwise; α_i^k are country-fixed effects; Time_t^k is a time trend; and β_k measures the impact of fiscal consolidation episodes on the change of the Gini coefficient for each future period k. Because fixed effects are included in the regression, the dynamic impact of consolidation episodes should be interpreted as changes in the Gini coefficient compared to a baseline country-specific trend.

Equation (T7) is estimated using the panel-corrected standard error (PCSE) estimator. This procedure is better placed to deal with the nature of our data (such as a small number of countries compared to the number of years) and to correct for panel-specific heteroskedasticity and serial correlation. The number of lags (l) has been chosen to be equal to 2, as this produces the best specification, but the results are extremely robust to different numbers of lags included in the specification (see robustness checks presented in the next section).

The dynamic responses of inequality to fiscal adjustments are then obtained by plotting the estimated β_k for $k = 0, 1 \ldots 8$, with confidence bands for the estimated effects being computed using the standard deviations associated with the estimated coefficients β_k. While the presence of a lagged dependent variable and country-fixed effects may in principle bias the estimation of γ_j^k and β_k in small samples, the length of the time dimension mitigates this concern. The finite sample bias is in the order of $1/T$, where T (total number of time periods) in our sample is 32.

Figure 6.3 shows the response of inequality to fiscal consolidation using the method described above. To assess the effects of fiscal consolidation on

the distribution of income between various groups, equation (T7) is also estimated for wage and profit income (figure 6.4), and for short-term and long-
term unemployment (figure 6.5).

Figure 7.1

To measure monetary policy shocks, we adapt the approach developed
by Auerbach and Gorodnichenko (2013) to identify fiscal policy shocks.
We proceed in two steps. First, using forecasts from *Consensus Economics*, we
compute unexpected changes in policy rates (proxied by short-term rates)
using the forecast error of the policy (short-term) rates (FE_t^i)—defined as
the difference between the actual policy short-term rates at the end of the
year (ST_t^r) and the rate expected by analysts as of the beginning of October
for the end of the same year (CT_t^r):

$$FE_{i,t}^r = ST_{i,t}^r - CT_{i,t}^r = \left(ST_{i,t}^r - ST_{i,t-1}^r \right) - (CT_{i,t}^r - ST_{i,t-1}^r) \qquad (T9)$$

We then regress for each country the forecast errors of the policy rates
(ST_t^r) on similarly computed forecast errors of inflation (FE^{inf}) and output
growth (FE^g):

$$FE_{i,t}^r = \alpha_i + \beta FE_{i,t}^{inf} + \gamma FE_{i,t}^g + \epsilon_{i,t} \qquad (T10)$$

where $FE_{i,t}^{inf} \left(FE_{i,t}^g \right)$ is the difference between the CPI inflation (GDP growth)
at the end of the year and the inflation (GDP growth) expected by analysts as
of the beginning of October for the end of the same year; the residuals—$\epsilon_{i,t}$
—capture exogenous monetary policy shocks. Monetary policy shocks are
identified for each country covered in *Consensus Economics*.

This methodology overcomes two problems that may otherwise confound
the causal estimation of the effect of monetary policy shocks on inequality. First, using forecast errors eliminates the problem of "policy foresight,"
namely that people may receive news about changes in monetary policy
in advance and may alter their consumption and investment behavior well
before the changes in policy occur. An econometrician who uses just the
information contained in the change in actual policy rate would be relying
on a smaller information set than that used by economic agents, leading to
inconsistent estimates of the effects of monetary policy shocks. In contrast,

by using forecast errors in policy rates, this methodology effectively aligns the economic agents' and the econometrician's information sets. Second, by purging news (that is, unexpected changes) in growth and inflation from the forecast errors in the short-term rate we significantly reduce the likelihood that the estimates capture the potentially endogenous response of monetary policy to changes in growth or inflation.

Figure 7.1 illustrates the measure of monetary policy shocks using our method for the United States and shows that it is quite similar to the popular measure of Romer and Romer (2004).

Figures 7.2, 7.3, 7.4, and 7.5

To estimate the impact of monetary policy shocks on inequality in the short and medium term, we follow the method proposed by Jordà (2005) discussed earlier, which consists of estimating impulse-response functions directly from local projections. Specifically, for each future period k the following equation is estimated on annual data:

$$y_{i,t+k} - y_{i,t} = \alpha_i^k + \vartheta_t^k + \beta^k MP_{i,t} + \pi^k X_{i,t} + \varepsilon_{i,t}^k \qquad (T11)$$

where y is the (log) of net income inequality; $MP_{i,t}$ are exogenous monetary policy shocks; α_i are country-fixed effects included to control for unobserved cross-country heterogeneity of inequality and also to control for the fact that in some countries inequality is measured using income data while in other countries using consumption data; ϑ_t are time-fixed effects to control for global shocks; X is a set of controls including lagged monetary policy shocks and lagged changes in inequality.

The baseline analysis focuses on net rather than gross income for two reasons. First, the source of data (the Luxembourg Income Study) through which gross market Gini data are computed in the SWIID dataset is based on household disposable income, and therefore is likely to be less subject to measurement errors. Second, we want to capture the overall effects of monetary policy shocks on inequality including through effects on redistribution (that is, tax and transfers). That said, the results based on market income are robust and not statistically different from those based on net income.

Equation (T10) is estimated for k=0, . . ., 4—that is, up to five years after the shock. Impulse-response functions are computed using the estimated coefficients β^k and the confidence intervals using the estimated standard errors of these coefficients. The sample period—determined by the availability of the series of monetary policy shocks and inequality—is from 1990 to 2013. The estimates for 32 advanced economies and emerging-market countries are based on clustered robust standard errors.

Figure 7.2 shows that our monetary policy shocks have the expected effects on macroeconomic variables such as output, inflation, and asset prices. The figures that follow show the impact of monetary policy shocks on the Gini measure of inequality (figure 7.3), the share of wage income (figure 7.4), and top income shares (figure 7.5).

GLOSSARY

Austerity *See* fiscal consolidation.

Capital account liberalization A process of opening up to foreign capital also referred to as financial openness, this process allows countries access to a deeper pool of capital and allows the owners of capital to search among a wider set of investment projects.

Cash transfer A direct transfer of income from rich to poor via government programs.

Current account liberalization Removing nontariff barriers to trade, such as keeping exchange systems free from restrictions on payments and transfers for current international transactions.

Deregulation A process of reducing and simplifying cumbersome government laws and procedures related to finance, trade, and labor, among others.

Domestic finance deregulation The decrease of controls on interest rates and credit, the increase of competition in the banking sector (i.e., number of banks and their market shares), and various aspects of the extent of development of financial markets.

Downbreak A period when growth slacks, which marks the end of a growth spell.

Easing monetary policy Reduction in interest rates targeted by the central bank.

Efficiency Term used by economists and others in the profession referring to economic growth (i.e., growth of the size of the pie).

Equity Term used by economists and others in the profession referring to the distribution of income (i.e., the size of the slice that goes to each person).

Exchange rate competitiveness Refers to the extent that a country's exchange rate is set at a rate favorable to its mix of exports and imports.

External debt Debt owed to foreign creditors.

Financial openness *See* capital account liberalization.

Fiscal consolidation Government policies that aim to reduce budget deficits, usually accomplished by combinations of spending cuts and tax hikes.

Foreign direct investment Investments made by foreign entities.

Gini index A measure of income inequality. The index is scaled so that it varies from 0–100: 0 means that all households receive the same income and 100 means that one household receives all the income.

Growth spell Long period of healthy growth marked by an upbreak and a downbreak.

Human capital The skills of the labor force in a given country.

Income inequality A concept referring to the extent that incomes are distributed in an uneven way.

Labor income share The amount of income going to labor (as opposed to capital) as a percent of all income.

Labor market reform Deregulation or changes in laws pertaining to issues of labor, such as changes in collective bargaining agreements.

Law and order The extent to which the legal system is impartial and the popular observance of the law.

Macro economic reforms A group of reforms that include policies by the finance (or treasury) ministries to keep the government's budget deficits—the gap between how much the government spends and how much it collects in taxes—from getting too large and by central banks to keep inflation in check.

Market Gini Measure of inequality before taxes and transfers.

Monetary policy Central banks' control of the supply of money by increasing or decreasing interest rates; this is usually done to achieve a target inflation rate and keep incomes close to their potential.

Net Gini Measure of inequality after taking into consideration taxes and transfers.

Openness to trade The extent that government policies are favorable toward trade. It is usually measured as the sum of exports and imports.

Political institution The structure of government, mainly concerned with the relationship between constituents and the executive and the level of accountability.

Predistribution Steps that are taken by governments in attempt to avoid extreme inequalities of income in the first place. These include providing more equal access to education and health care. These policies raise the odds that the poor and their children would end with high incomes despite the disadvantages of their initial starting points in life.

Redistribution A process of transferring income from the rich to the poor, usually accomplished by taxing the rich at a progressively higher rate than the poor and/or by giving the poor cash transfers and other social benefits (e.g., food stamps and welfare payments).

Structural reforms A broad group or reforms, which include being open to international trade and flows of foreign capital, avoiding excessive regulation of product and labor markets, and adopting policies to deregulate the financial sector.

Tariff Tax on imports. Higher taxes on imports translate to less openness to trade.

Top income share The amount of income going to the rich (this can vary, such as the top 0.1 percent, 1 percent, or 10 percent) as a percent of all income.

Upbreak A period in which growth takes off, which marks the beginning of a growth spell.

REFERENCES

Abiad, Abdul, Enrica Detragiache, and Thierry Tressel. 2008. "A New Database of Financial Reforms," *IMF Working Paper* 08/266 International Monetary Fund, Washington, D.C.

Abiad, Abdul, and Ashoka Mody. 2005. "Financial Reform: What Shakes It? What Shapes It?" *American Economic Review*, 95 (1): 66–88.

Acemoglu, Daron, and Simon Johnson. 2012. "Who Captured the Fed?" *The New York Times*, March 29, 2012. https://economix.blogs.nytimes.com/2012/03/29/who-captured-the-fed/?_r=0.

Adhikari, Bibek, Romain Duval, Bingjie Hu, and Prakash Loungani. 2018. "Can Reform Waves Turn the Tide? Some Case Studies Using the Synthetic Control Method." *Open Economies Review*: 1–32.

Aerts, J.J., Denis Cogneau, Javier Herrera, G. de Monchy, and François Roubaud. 2000. *L'économie camerounaise: Un espoir évanoui*. Paris: Karthala.

Aghion, Philippe, Eve Caroli, and Cecilia García-Peñalosa. 1999. "Inequality and Economic Growth: The Perspective of the New Growth Theories." *Journal of Economic Literature* 37 (4): 1615–660.

Alesina, Alberto, and Dani Rodrik. 1994. "Distributive Politics and Economic Growth." *The Quarterly Journal of Economics* 109 (2): 465–90.

Alesina, Alberto, and Roberto Perotti. 1996. "Income Distribution, Political Instability, and Investment." *European Economic Review* 40 (6): 1203–228.

Alesina, Alberto, Enrico Spolaore, and Romain Wacziarg. 2005. "Trade, Growth and the Size of Countries." In *Handbook of Economic Growth*, ed. Philippe Aghion and Steven Durlauf, 1499–542: North Holland, Amsterdam.

Árvai, Zsófia. 2005. "Capital Account Liberalization, Capital Flow Patterns, and Policy Responses in the EU's New Member States." *IMF Working Papers* 05/213 (1). https://doi.org/10.5089/9781451862324.001.

Atkinson, Anthony B., Thomas Piketty, and Emmanuel Saez. 2011. "Top Incomes in the Long Run of History." *Journal of Economic Literature* 49 (1): 3–71.

Atkinson, Anthony, and Maria Lugo. 2014. "Growth, Poverty and Distribution in Tanzania." *IGC International Growth Centre* (blog). January 7, 2014.

Auerbach, Alan, and Yuriy Gorodnichenko. 2013a. "Fiscal Multipliers in Recession and Expansion." In *Fiscal Policy After the Financial Crisis*, eds. Alberto Alesina and Francesco Giavazzi. Cambridge, Massachusetts: NBER Books, National Bureau of Economic Research, Inc.

——. 2013b. "Measuring the Output Responses to Fiscal Policy." *American Economic Journal: Economic Policy* 4 (2): 1–27.

Auriol, Emmanuelle. 2005. "Telecommunication Reforms in Developing Countries." *Communications & Strategies*, Special Issue (November 2005): 31–53.

Autor, David H. 2015. "Why Are There Still So Many Jobs? The History and Future of Workplace Automation." *Journal of Economic Perspectives* 29 (3): 3–30.

Bai J., and P. Perron. 1998. "Estimating and testing linear models with multiple structural changes." *Econometrica* 66: 47–78.

——. 2003. "Computation and analysis of multiple structural change models." *Journal of Applied Econometrics* 18: 1–22. doi:10.1002/jae.659.

Baldacci, Emanuele, Iva Petrova, Nazim Belhocine, Gabriela Dobrescu, and Samah Mazraani. 2011. "Assessing Fiscal Stress." *IMF Working Papers* 11/100.

Ball, Laurence, Daniel Leigh, and Prakash Loungani. 2011. "Painful Medicine." *Finance & Development* 48 (3): 20–23.

Ball, Laurence M., Davide Furceri, Daniel Leigh, and Prakash Loungani. 2013. "The Distributional Effects of Fiscal Consolidation." *IMF Working Papers* 12/151. https://doi.org/10.5089/9781475551945.001.

Barro, Robert. 2000. "Inequality and Growth in a Panel of Countries." *Journal of Economic Growth* 5 (2): 5–32.

Barro, Robert and Jong-Wha Lee, 2013, "A New Data Set of Educational Attainment in the World, 1950–2010." *Journal of Development Economics* 104: 84–198.

Benabou, Roland. 2000. "Unequal Societies: Income Distribution and the Social Contract." *American Economic Review* 90 (1): 96–129.

Benhabib, Jess. 2003. "The Tradeoff Between Inequality and Growth." *Annals of Economics and Finance* 4: 329–45.

Berg, Andrew, Edward Buffie, and Luis-Felipe Zanna. 2018. "Robots, Growth, and Inequality: Should We Fear the Robot Revolution?" *Journal of Monetary Economics*, forthcoming. https://www.sciencedirect.com/science/article /pii/S0304393218302204.

Berg, Andrew, and Jonathan D. Ostry. 2012. "How Inequality Damages Economies." *Foreign Affairs*. https://www.foreignaffairs.com/articles/2012-01-06 /how-inequality-damages-economies.

——. 2017. "Inequality and Unsustainable Growth: Two Sides of the Same Coin?" *IMF Economic Review* 65 (4): 792–815.

Berg, Andrew, Jonathan D. Ostry, and Jeromin Zettelmeyer. 2012. "What Makes Growth Sustained?" *Journal of Development Economics* 95 (2): 149–66. https://doi.org/10.1016/j.jdeveco.2011.08.002.

Berg, Andrew, and Jeffrey Sachs. 1988. "The Debt Crisis: Structural Explanations of Country Performance." *National Bureau of Economic Research*. https://doi.org/10.3386/w2607.

Bernanke, Ben. 2015. "Monetary Policy and Inequality 3." Brookings website, June 1, 2015. https://www.brookings.edu/blog/ben-bernanke/2015/06/01 /monetary-policy-and-inequality/.

Blanchard, Olivier, Jonathan D. Ostry, Atish Ghosh, and Marcos Chamon. 2016. "Capital Flows: Expansionary or Contractionary?" *American Economic Review* 106 (5): 565–69.

——. 2017. "Are Capital Inflows Expansionary or Contractionary?" *IMF Economic Review*, 65 (3): 563–85.

Boushey, Heather, and Carter Price. 2014. "How are Economic Inequality and Growth Connected? A Review of Recent Research." Washington Center for Equitable Growth.

Cameron, David. 2011. "Speech to World Economic Forum Annual Meeting 2011." *New Statesman*. Accessed January 4, 2017. http://www.newstatesman .com/economy/2011/01/europe-world-growth-values.

Čapek, Karel. 1921. *R.U.R. (Rossum's Universal Robots)*. New York: Penguin.

Carbonnier, Gilles. 2002. "The Competing Agendas of Economic Reform and Peace Process: A Politico-Economic Model Applied to Guatemala." *World Development* 30 (8): 1323–339. https://doi.org/10.1016/s0305-750 x(02)00041-4.

Cárdenas, Mauricio. 2007. "Economic Growth in Colombia: A Reversal Of 'Fortune'?" *Banco de la Republica* 25 (53): 220–59.

Center for Systemic Peace. "Polity IV Database." Accessed January 5, 2017. http://www.systemicpeace.org/inscrdata.html.

Chinn, Menzie D., and Hiro Ito. 2006. "What Matters for Financial Development? Capital Controls, Institutions, and Interactions." *Journal of Development Economics* 81 (1): 163–92. https://doi.org/10.1016/j.jdeveco.2005.05.010.

Coibion, Olivier, Yuriy Gorodnichenko, Lorenz Kueng, and John Silvia. 2012. "Innocent Bystanders? Monetary Policy and Inequality in the U.S." *NBER Working Paper* 18170. National Bureau of Economic Research, Inc.

Conley, Tom. 2004. "Globalisation and Rising Inequality in Australia: Is Increasing Inequality Inevitable in Australia?" Griffith University.

Dao, Mai, and Prakash Loungani. 2010. "The Human Cost of Recessions: Assessing It, Reducing It." IMF Staff Position Note 10/17.

Dell'Ariccia, Giovanni, Paolo Mauro, Andre Faria, Jonathan D. Ostry, Julian Di Giovanni, Martin Schindler, Ayhan Kose, and Marco Terrones. 2008. "Reaping the Benefits of Financial Globalization." *IMF Occasional Paper* 264. https://doi.org/10.5089/9781589067486.084.

Demirguc-Kunt, Asli; Klapper, Leora; Singer, Dorothe; Van Oudheusden, Peter. 2015. "The Global Findex Database 2014: measuring financial inclusion around the world." *Policy Research working paper; no. WPS 7255*. Washington, D.C.: World Bank Group.

DeVries, Pete, Jaime Guajardo, Daniel Leigh, and Andrea Pescatori. 2011. "A New Action-based Dataset of Fiscal Consolidation." *IMF Working Papers* 11/128. International Monetary Fund, Washington, D.C.

Draghi, Mario. 2016. "Reviving the Spirit of De Gasperi: Working Together for an Effective and Inclusive Union." European Central Bank. Accessed December 28, 2017. https://www.ecb.europa.eu/press/key/date/2016/html/sp160913.en.html.

Dreher, Axel. 2006. "Does Globalization Affect Growth? Evidence from a New Index of Globalization." *Applied Economics* 38 (10): 1091–110. https://doi.org/10.1080/00036840500392078.

Fischer, Stanley. 1997. *Capital Account Liberalization and the Role of the IMF*. Washington, D.C.: International Monetary Fund.

Ford, Martin. 2015. *The Rise of the Robots*. New York: Basic Books.

Frankel, Jeffrey, and David Romer. 1999. "Does Trade Cause Growth?" *American Economic Review* 89 (3): 379–99.

Freeman, Richard B. 2015. "Who Owns the Robots Rules the World." IZA World of Labor.

Frey, Carl Benedikt, and Michael A. Osborne. 2013. "The Future of Employment: How Susceptible Are Jobs to Computerisation?" Oxford University paper. Oxford: United Kingdom.

Friedman, Milton. 1982. "Free Markets and the Generals." Accessed January 5, 2017. http://miltonfriedman.hoover.org/objects/56785/free-markets-and-the-generals;jsessionid=38A8010F72B94DF404B43DEAB9544B0F.

Furceri, Davide, and Prakash Loungani. 2017. "Capital Account Liberalization and Inequality." *Journal of Development Economics* 130: 127–144.

Furceri, Davide, Jun Ge, and Prakash Loungani. 2016. "Financial Liberalization, Inequality and Inclusion in Low-Income Countries." *Dynamic Modeling and Econometrics in Economics and Finance* 23. https://doi.org/10.1007/978-3-319-54690-2_4.

Furceri, Davide, Prakash Loungani, and Jonathan D. Ostry. 2018. "The Aggregate and Distributional Effects of Financial Globalization." *IMF Working Paper. 18/83*. International Monetary Fund, Washington D.C.

Furceri, Davide, Prakash Loungani, and Aleksandra Zdzienicka. 2017. "The Effects of Monetary Policy Shocks on Inequality." *Journal of International Money and Finance* 85: 168–86.

Galbraith, James. 2016. *Inequality: What Everyone Needs to Know*. Oxford University Press.

Galor, Oded, and Omer Moav. 2004. "From Physical to Human Capital Accumulation: Inequality and the Process of Development." *Review of Economic Studies* 71: 1001–026.

Galor, Oded, and Joseph Zeira. 1993. "Income Distribution and Macroeconomics." *The Review of Economics Studies* 60 (1): 32–52.

Galperin, Hernan. 2005. "Telecommunications reforms and the poor: the case of Argentina." Paper presented at the seminar Digital Divides: Best Practices and False Perceptions, Oxford Internet Institute. March 4, 2005.

Ghosh, Atish, Jun Kim, Enrique Mendoza, Jonathan D. Ostry, and Mahvash Qureshi. 2013. "Fiscal Fatigue, Fiscal Space and Debt Sustainability in Advanced Economies." *The Economic Journal* 123(566): F4–F30.

Ghosh, Atish, Jonathan D. Ostry, and Mahvash Qureshi. 2013. "Fiscal Space and Sovereign Risk Pricing in a Currency Union." *Journal of International Money and Finance* 34: 131–63.

——. 2016. "When Do Capital Inflow Surges End in Tears?" *American Economic Review* 106 (5): 581–85. https://doi.org/10.1257/aer.p20161015.

——. 2017. *Taming the Tide of Capital Flows*. Cambridge, MA: MIT Press.

Goldin, Ian, and Kenneth A. Reinert. 2012. *Globalization for Development: Meeting New Challenges*. Oxford: Oxford University Press.

Greenville, Jared, Clinton Pobke, and Nikki Rogers. 2013. *Trends in the Distribution of Income in Australia*. Melbourne, Victoria: Productivity Commission.

Greenwood, Jeremy, and Boyan Jovanovic. 1990. "Financial Development, Growth, and the Distribution of Income." *The Journal of Political Economy* 98 (5) Part 1: 1076–107.

Guriev, Sergei, Danny Leipziger, and Jonathan D. Ostry. 2017. "Making Globalisation More Inclusive: A Way Forward." *VoxEu.* http://voxeu.org/article/making-globalisation-more-inclusive.

Gwartney, James, Robert Lawson, and Joshua Hall. 2017. Economic Freedom of the World: 2017 Annual Report. Fraser Institute

Gygli, Savina, Florian Haelg, and Jan-Egbert Sturm. 2018. "The KOF Globalization Index—Revisited." *KOF Working Paper No. 439.* KOF Swiss Economic Institute, ETH Zurich.

Hausmann, Ricardo, Lant Pritchett, and Dani Rodrik. 2005. "Growth Accelerations." *Journal of Economic Growth* 10 (4): 303–29. https://doi.org/10.1007/s10887-005-4712-0.

Heath, Allister. 2015. "A Return to Capital Controls Would Be a Disaster for All of Us." *The Telegraph*, February 20, 2015. http://www.telegraph.co.uk/finance/economics/11426309/A-return-to-capital-controls-would-be-a-disaster-for-all-of-us.html.

Howell, Tom Jr. 2013. "IMF Chief: U.S. Dance with the Debt Limit Is 'very, very concerning.' " *Washington Times*, October 13, 2013, https://www.washingtontimes.com/news/2013/oct/13/imf-chief-us-dance-debt-limit-very-very-concerning/.

International Monetary Fund. "AREAER Online." IMF eLibrary. Accessed January 5, 2017. http://www.elibrary.imf.org.

Jácome, Luis Ignacio, Carlos Larrea M., and Rob Vos. 1998. *Políticas macroeconómicas, distribución y pobreza en el Ecuador*. Quito, Ecuador: CORDES.

Jayadev, Arjun. 2005. "Financial Liberalization and Its Distributional Consequences: An Empirical Exploration." Dissertation: University of Massachusetts—Amherst.

——. 2007. "Capital Account Openness and the Labour Share of Income." *Cambridge Journal of Economics* 31 (3): 423–43. https://doi.org/10.1093/cje/bel037.

Jordà, Òscar. 2005. "Estimation and Inference of Impulse Responses by Local Projections." *American Economic Review*, 95 (1): 161–182.

Kuznets, Simon. 1955. "Economic Growth and Income Inequality." *American Economic Review* 45 (1): 1–28.

Laeven, Luc, and Fabian Valencia. 2010. "Resolution of Banking Crises: The Good, the Bad, and the Ugly." *IMF Working Papers* 10/146. International Monetary Fund, Washington D.C.

Lagarde, Christine. 2014. "The Caribbean and the IMF—Building a Partnership for the Future." Speech delivered at the University of the West Indies at Mona, Jamaica, June 27, 2014. https://www.imf.org/en/News/Articles/2015/09/28/04/53/sp062714.

Lagarde, Christine. 2015. "Ethics and Finance—Aligning Financial Incentives with Societal Objectives", speech delivered at "Conversation with Janet Yellen, Chair of the Board of Governors of the Federal Reserve System," the Institute for New Economic Thinking, May 6, 2015, Washington D.C.

Lane, Philip R., and Gian Maria Milesi-Ferretti. 2007. "The External Wealth of Nations Mark II: Revised and Extended Estimates of Foreign Assets and Liabilities, 1970–2004." *Journal of International Economics* 73 (2): 223–50. https://doi.org/10.1016/j.jinteco.2007.02.003.

Lazear, Edward, and Sherwin Rosen. 1981. "Rank-Order Tournaments as Optimum Labor Contracts." *Journal of Political Economy* 89 (5): 841–64.

Lewis, Peter. 2007. *Growing Apart: Oil, Politics, and Economic Change in Indonesia and Nigeria*. Ann Arbor: University of Michigan Press.

Lindert, Peter. 2004. *Growing Public: Volume 1, The Story: Social Spending and Economic Growth Since the Eighteenth Century*. Cambridge: Cambridge University Press.

Lipton, David. 2016. "A Two-Way Street." *Finance and Development*, 53 (4): 17.

Loungani, Prakash. 2017. "The Power of Two: Inclusive Growth and the IMF"." *Intereconomics* 52 (2), 92–9. (See also "Inclusive Growth and the IMF," IMF Blog, January 24, 2017.)

Lucas, Robert E., Jr. 1988. "On the Mechanics of Economic Development." *Journal of Monetary Economics* 22 (1): 3–42.

——. 2003. "The Industrial Revolution: Past and Future." Federal Reserve Bank of Minnesota, Annual Report Essay.

Mbaku, John Mukum, and Joseph Takougang. 2003. *The Leadership Challenge in Africa: Cameroon Under Paul Biya*. Trenton, New Jersey: Africa World Press.

McCloskey, Deirdre N. 2016. "Growth, Not Forced Equality, Saves the Poor." *The New York Times*, December 23, 2016. http://www.nytimes.com/2016/12/23/business/growth-not-forced-equality-saves-the-poor.html.

McKenzie, David, and Dilip Mookherjee. 2003. "The Distributive Impact of Privatization in Latin America: Evidence from Four Countries." *Economía* 3: 161–218. https://doi.org/10.1353/eco.2003.0006.

McLeod, Ross H. 1994. *Indonesia Assessment 1994: Finance as a Key Sector in Indonesia's Development*. Canberra: Research School of Pacific and Asian Studies, Australian National University.

Meltzer, Allan H., and Scott F. Richard. 1981. "A Rational Theory of the Size of Government." *The Journal of Political Economy* 89 (5): 914–27.

Mendoza, Enrique, and Jonathan D. Ostry. 2008. "International Evidence on Fiscal Solvency: Is Fiscal Policy 'Responsible'?" *Journal of Monetary Economics* 55 (6): 1081–093.

Milanovic, Branko. 2005. *Worlds Apart: Measuring International and Global Inequality.* Princeton, NJ: Princeton University Press.

——. 2016. *Global Inequality: A New Approach for the Age of Globalization.* Cambridge, MA: The Belknap Press (Harvard University Press).

Nakajima, Makoto. 2015. "The Redistributive Consequences of Monetary Policy." Federal Reserve Bank of Philadelphia. Accessed June 1, 2017. https://www.philadelphiafed.org/-/media/research-and-data/publications /business-review/2015/q2/brQ215_the_redistributive_consequences_of _monetary_policy.pdf.

Obama, Barack. 2011. "Remarks by the President on the Economy in Osawatomie, Kansas." The White House, obamawhitehouse.archives.gov/the-press -office/2011/12/06/remarks-president-economy-osawatomie-kansas. Accessed December 27, 2017.

Obstfeld, Maurice. 1998. "The Global Capital Market: Benefactor or Menace?" *Journal of Economic Perspectives* 12 (4): 9–30. https://doi.org/10.1257 /jep.12.4.9.

——. 2016. "Get on Track with Trade." *Finance & Development* 53 (4): 12–16.

Obstfeld, Maurice, Jonathan D. Ostry, and Mahvash Qureshi. 2018. "A Tie that Binds: Revisiting the Trilemma in Emerging Market Economies." *American Economic Review* 108 (5).

Okun, Arthur M. 1975. *Equality and Efficiency, the Big Tradeoff.* Washington: Brookings Institution.

Ostry, Jonathan D. 2012. "Managing Capital Flows: What Tools to Use?" *Asian Development Review* 29 (1): 83–89.

——. 2014. "We Do Not Have to Live with the Scourge of Inequality." *Financial Times.* March 3, 2014.

——. 2015. "Inequality and the Duration of Growth." *European Journal of Economics and Economic Policies* 12 (2): 147–57.

Ostry, Jonathan D., and Andrew Berg. 2014. "Measure to Measure." *Finance & Development* 51 (3): 35–38.

Ostry, Jonathan D., Andrew Berg, and Siddharth Kothari. 2018. "Growth-Equity Trade-offs in Structural Reforms?" *IMF Working Paper* No. 18/5. International Monetary Fund, Washington D.C.

Ostry, Jonathan D., Andrew Berg, and Charalambos Tsangarides. 2014. "Redistribution, Inequality, and Growth." *Staff Discussion Notes* 14 (2): 1. https://doi.org/10.5089/9781484352076.006. Forthcoming, *Journal of Economic Growth*. (See also " Redistribution, Inequality, and Sustainable Growth: Reconsidering the Evidence." *VoxEu*. http://voxeu.org/article/redistribution-inequality-and-sustainable-growth.)

Ostry, Jonathan D., Atish Ghosh, and Raphael Espinoza. 2015. "When Should Public Debt Be Reduced?" *Staff Discussion Notes* 15 (10): 1. https://doi.org/10.5089/9781498379205.006. (See also "Don't Sweat the Debt if Fiscal Space is Ample." *VoxEu*. http://voxeu.org/article/don-t-sweat-debt-if-fiscal-space-ample.)

Ostry, Jonathan D., Atish Ghosh, Marcos Chamon, and Mahvash Qureshi. 2011. "Capital Controls: When and Why?" *IMF Economic Review* 59 (3): 562–80.

——. 2012. "Tools for Managing Financial-Stability Risks from Capital Inflows," *Journal of International Economics* 88 (2): 407–21.

Ostry, Jonathan D., Atish Ghosh, and Mahvash Qureshi. 2015. *Capital Controls*. Edward Elgar Publishing (The International Library of Critical Writings in Economics 308).

Ostry, Jonathan D., Prakash Loungani, and Davide Furceri. 2016. "Neoliberalism: Oversold?" *Finance & Development* 53 (2): 38–41.

Ostry, Jonathan D., Prakash Loungani, and Davide Furceri. 2018. "Are New Economic Policy Rules Desirable to Mitigate Rising National Inequalities?" In *International Policy Rules and Inequality: Implications for Global Economic Governance*, ed. José Antonio Ocampo (Columbia University Press, New York).

Ostry, Jonathan D., Alessandro Prati, and Spilimbergo, Antonio. 2009. "Structural Reforms and Economic Performance in Advanced and Developing Countries." *IMF Occasional Paper No. 268*. https://doi.org/10.5089/9781589068186.084.

Perotti, Roberto, 1996. "Growth, Income Distribution, and Democracy: What the Data Say," *Journal of Economic Growth* 1 (2): 149–87.

Piketty, Thomas, Emmanuel Saez, and Gabriel Zucman. 2016. "Economic Growth in the United States: A Tale of Two Countries." *Equitable Growth*. Accessed January 3, 2017. http://equitablegrowth.org/research-analysis/economic-growth-in-the-united-states-a-tale-of-two-countries/.

Pope Francis. 2014. "Address of Pope Francis to the UN System Chief Executive Board for Coordination." The Vatican, http://w2.vatican.va/content/francesco/en/speeches/2014/may.index.2.html.

Pritchett, Lant. 2000. "Understanding Patterns of Economic Growth: Searching for Hills Among Plateaus, Mountains, and Plains." *The World Bank Economic Review* 14 (2): 221–50. https://doi.org/10.1093/wber/14.2.221.

Quinn, Dennis. 1997. "The Correlates of Change in International Financial Regulation." *American Political Science Review* 91 (3): 531–51. https://doi.org/10.2307/2952073.

Quinn, Dennis, and A. Maria Toyoda. 2008. "Does Capital Account Liberalization Lead to Growth?" *Review of Financial Studies* 21 (3): 1403–449. https://doi.org/10.1093/rfs/hhn034.

Rajan, Raghuram, 2011. *Fault Lines: How Hidden Fractures Still Threaten the World Economy*. Princeton, NJ: Princeton University Press.

Rajan, Raghuram G., and Luigi Zingales. 1998. "Financial Dependence and Growth." *The American Economic Review* 88 (3): 559–86.

Reinhart Carmen M., and Kenneth S. Rogoff. 2010. "Growth in a Time of Debt." *American Economic Review*, 100 (2): 573–78.

Rodrik, Dani. 1997. *Has Globalization Gone Too Far?* Washington, D.C.: Peterson Institute for International Economics.

——. 1998. "Who Needs Capital-Account Convertibility?" *Essays in International Finance* 207.

——. 1999. "Where Did All the Growth Go? External Shocks, Social Conflict, and Growth Collapses." *Journal of Economic Growth* 4 (4): 385–412 (a).

——. 1999. "Institutions for High-Quality Growth: What They are and How to Acquire Them." *IMF Conference on Second Generation Reforms*. https://doi.org/10.3386/w7540 (b).

——. 2008. "The Real Exchange Rate and Economic Growth." *Brookings Papers on Economic Activity*. 2008 (2): 365–412.

Romer, Christina D., and David H. Romer. 2004. "A New Measure of Monetary Shocks: Derivation and Implications." *American Economic Review* 94 (4): 1055–084. https://doi.org/10.1257/0002828042002651.

Ropp, Steve C. 1992. "Explaining the Long-Term Maintenance of a Military Regime: Panama Before the U.S. Invasion." *World Politics* 44 (2): 210–34. https://doi.org/10.2307/2010447.

Sachs, Jeffrey, and Laurence Kotlikoff. 2012. "Smart Machines and Long-Term Misery." *NBER Working Paper No. 18629*. National Bureau of Economic Research. Cambridge, Massachusetts. http://www.nber.org/papers/w18629.

Sachs, Jeffrey, and Andrew Warner. 1995. "Natural Resource Abundance and Economic Growth." *NBER Working Paper No. 5398*. National Bureau of Economic Research. Cambridge, Massachusetts. http://www.nber.org/papers/w5398.

Saint-Paul, Gilles, and Thierry Verdier. 1993. "Education, Democracy and Growth." *Journal of Development Economics* 42 (2): 399–407.

———. 1997. "Power, Distributive Conflicts, and Multiple Growth Paths." *Journal of Economic Growth* 2 (2): 155–68.

Samuelson, Robert. 2013. "Capitalists Wait, While Labor Loses Out," *The Washington Post*, September 8, 2013.

Schiffrin, Anya. 2016. "Capital Controls." New York: Initiative for Policy Dialogue.

Sokoloff, Kenneth L., and Stanley L. Engerman. 2000. "History Lessons: Institutions, Factors Endowments, and Paths of Development in the New World." *Journal of Economic Perspectives* 14 (3): 217–32.

Solt, Frederick. 2009. "Standardizing the World Income Inequality Database." *Social Science Quarterly* 90 (2): 231–42. https://doi.org/10.1111/j.1540 -6237.2009.00614.x.

Stiglitz, Joseph. 2002. "The Chilean Miracle: Combining Markets with Appropriate Reform." *Commanding Heights* interview.

———. 2012. *The Price of Inequality: How Today's Divided Society Endangers Our Future.* New York: Norton.

———. 2015. *The Great Divide: Unequal Societies and What We Can Do About Them.* New York: Norton.

Svejnar, Jan. 2002. "Transition Economies: Performance and Challenges." *Journal of Economic Perspectives* 16 (1): 3–28.

Tanzi, Vito, and Howell H. Zee. 1997. "Fiscal Policy and Long-Run Growth." *Staff Papers (International Monetary Fund)* 44 (2): 179–209.

Solt, Frederick. 2016. "The Standardized World Income Inequality Database." *Social Science Quarterly* 97 (5): 1267–81.

Thorp, Rosemary, Corinne Caumartin, and George Gray-Molina. 2006. "Inequality, Ethnicity, Political Mobilisation and Political Violence in Latin America: The Cases of Bolivia, Guatemala and Peru." *Bulletin of Latin American Research* 25 (4): 453–80. https://doi.org/10.1111/j.1470-9856.2006.00207.x.

Treichel, Volker. 2005. "Tanzania's Growth Process and Success in Reducing Poverty." *IMF Working Papers* 5 (35): 1. International Monetary Fund. Washington D.C. https://doi.org/10.5089/9781451860542.001.

Tsui, Kai-Yuen. 1996. "Economic Reform and Interprovincial Inequalities in China." *Journal of Development Economics* 50 (2): 353–68. https://doi .org/10.1016/s0304-3878(96)00406-3.

Voinea, Liviu, and Pierre Monnin. 2017. "Inequality Should Matter for Central Banks." *Council on Economic Policies.* Accessed June 1, 2017. https://www .cepweb.org/inequality-should-matter-for-central-banks/.

Wacziarg, Romain, and Karen Horn Welch. 2007. "Trade Liberalization and Growth: New Evidence." *The World Bank Economic Review* 22 (2): 187–231. https://doi.org/10.1093/wber/lhn007.

Wilkinson, Richard G., and Kate Pickett. 2011. *The Spirit Level: Why Greater Equality Makes Societies Stronger*. New York: Bloomsbury.

Woo, Jaejoon, Elva Bova, Tidiane Kinda, and Y. Sophia Zhang. 2017. "Distributional Consequences of Fiscal Adjustments: What Do the Data Say?" *IMF Economic Review* 65 (2): 273–307.

World Bank. 1993. *The East Asian Miracle: Economic Growth and Public Policy*. World Bank Policy Research Report.

Yang, Dennis Tao. 1999. "Urban-Biased Policies and Rising Income Inequality in China." *American Economic Review* 89 (2): 306–10. https://doi.org/10.1257/aer.89.2.306.

Yellen, Janet. 2014. "Perspectives on Inequality and Opportunity from the Survey of Consumer Finances." Speech at the Conference on Economic Opportunity and Inequality, Federal Reserve Bank of Boston, October 17, 2014. https://www.federalreserve.gov/newsevents/speech/yellen20141017a.htm.

INDEX

Page numbers in *italics* indicate figures or tables

JONATHAN D. OSTRY is deputy director of the research department at the International Monetary Fund, where his work on financial globalization and inequality has been influential in bringing about a shift in the IMF's stance on these issues. His many books include *Taming the Tide of Capital Flows* (2017). His work on inequality and unsustainable growth has been cited by, among others, Barack Obama. He has published widely on international macroeconomic issues in scholarly journals, and his work has received widespread attention in the press, including the *Economist, the Financial Times*, the *Wall Street Journal*, the *New York Times*, and the *Washington Post*. He is listed in *Who's Who in Economics* (2003). Ostry received his BA (with distinction) from Queen's University (Canada), where he was an undergraduate medalist, at the age of 18. He earned another BA from Oxford University (Balliol College) as a Commonwealth Scholar in Philosophy, Politics and Economics, followed by an MSc at the London School of Economics, and a PhD in economics at the University of Chicago. At the IMF, Ostry has been involved in efforts to raise awareness of inequality issues at the global level, including through his membership in the World Economic Forum's global agenda councils on inclusive growth, and through his writings on neoliberal policies, which have received widespread attention.

PRAKASH LOUNGANI is assistant director in the IMF's Independent Evaluation Office. Known for his work on promoting inclusive growth, he blogs as *The Unassuming Economist*. He has served on the World Economic Forum's global agenda councils on employment. He has been an adjunct professor of management at Vanderbilt University's Owen School of Management since 2001 and previously worked at the Federal Reserve Board.

ANDREW BERG is deputy director of the IMF's Institute for Capacity Development. He previously served at the U.S. Treasury, including as deputy assistant secretary for East Asia and Latin America in 2000–2001 and chief economist of the Mexican Task Force in 1995–96.